CHRISTOPH. COLVMB.

COLUMBUS
FOR GOLD · GOD · AND GLORY

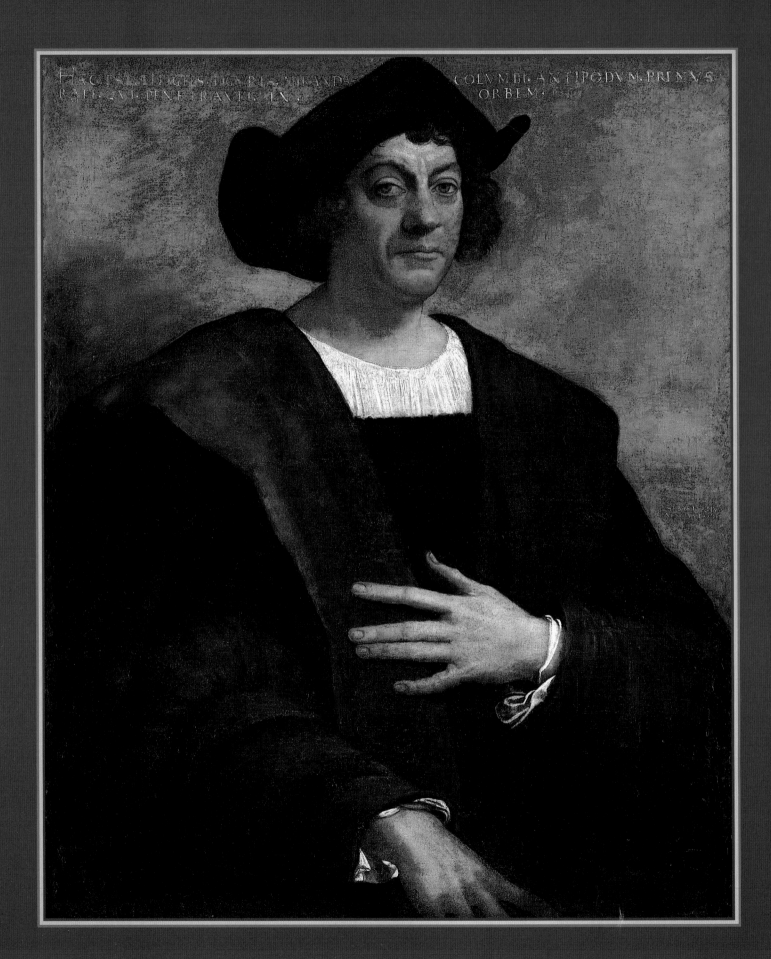

COLUMBUS
FOR GOLD · GOD · AND GLORY

TEXT BY

JOHN DYSON

PHOTOGRAPHS BY

PETER CHRISTOPHER, R.C.A.

NAUTICAL RESEARCH BY

DR. LUÍS MIGUEL COIN CUENCA

A SIMON & SCHUSTER / MADISON PRESS BOOK

New York   London   Toronto   Sydney   Tokyo   Singapore

SIMON AND SCHUSTER

Simon & Schuster Building, Rockefeller Center,
1230 Avenue of the Americas, New York, NY 10020

First published in the United States of America by Simon & Schuster Inc.

*SIMON AND SCHUSTER and colophon are registered trademarks
of Simon & Schuster Inc.*

Library of Congress Cataloguing
in Publication Data

Dyson, John, 1943-
Columbus: for gold, God and glory/text by John Dyson:
photographs by Peter Christopher;
nautical research by Luís Miguel Coin Cuenca

p.228cm.

ISBN 0-671-68791-3
1. Columbus, Christopher. 2. America—discovery and exploration—Spanish.
I. Christopher, Peter. II. Coin Cuenca, Luís Miguel. III. Title.
E111.D97 1991 970.01'5—dc20 90-23197 CIP

Produced by Madison Press Books
40 Madison Avenue, Toronto, Ontario, Canada M5R 2S1

Printed in Italy

For our families:

Kate,

Jemima, Jenny,

Jack and Kinna

in Barnes,

London, England

and

Suzanne,

Adam and Lucas

in Spring Brook,

Ontario, Canada

CONTENTS

1 THE SECRET OF COLUMBUS

Sailing in the Wake of History

The boom of a farewell cannon rebounded from the cliffs enclosing the tiny harbor of Gomera in the Canary Islands. Like a medieval phantom, the *Niña* emerged from the smoke and turned toward the open Atlantic. Her sails, bellying in the breeze, were tamed and trimmed by rope-chafed hands. A white wave began to bubble around the caravel's blunt black bow. The flag of Castile rippled from the mainmast, and Columbus's own banner flew from the mizzen. From forward drifted the aroma of lentil soup which, with hard bread, blood sausage and beans, would be our staple fare during the weeks of tough sea voyaging ahead. It was a Saturday morning in June 1990, and we were bound on a 2,700-mile historical odyssey.

Soon the *Niña* was swooping through a disheveled wilderness of foaming blue seas, her wake a crooked finger pointing at our last sight of the Old World. The trade wind breezed over the poop, and sunlight speared through the lace holes of swelling sails. As authentic as lack of technology could make her, our sixty-four-foot replica of a medieval caravel was powered only by rope, spar and canvas, and by the sinew and nerve of eighteen nautical students from the University of Cadiz in Spain. Like Columbus's men long ago, many of our hapless crew were discovering that seasickness has two stages: the first when you think you are going to die and the second when you hope you will.

Scattering flying fish as she surged through twenty-foot waves, the caravel was part of a world that was still exactly as Christopher Columbus had seen it nearly five centuries before. Like the original *Niña*—the smallest ship of his fleet and his favorite—our replica was rugged, low to the water and uncomfortable. Painted inside and out with pitch, she was a black country of tar that went soft and sticky in the sun. Like Columbus's men we sought a soft plank to sleep on, crowding into a dark and dank hold where nobody could stand upright. We had neither engine nor electronic navigation aids, and only a candle illuminated our compass. We gulped water from earthen jars, and the sea was our only bathroom. While hanging over the side on a rope to visit what the chroniclers of Columbus's time termed "the house of necessities," a roll of the ship would often dip us to the waist.

By sailing in the wake of Columbus and reliving as closely as possible the conditions and experiences of his remarkable voyage, all of us on board the *Niña* aimed to contribute to a whole new understanding of the maritime skills, motivations and even the enigmatic character of history's most famous navigator. Our captain was Dr. Luís Coin Cuenca, a former ship's officer who was now a professor of maritime history. After painstaking analysis of nautical clues in fifteenth-century records, Dr. Coin had determined that many of the traditional notions of how Columbus discovered the New World were wrong.

After Jesus Christ, no individual has made a bigger impact on the Western world than Christopher Columbus. He is commemorated in the names given to streets, cities, rivers and even in the name of a country, yet the reason he dared to embark on his fateful enterprise has never been adequately explained. Although academics have scrutinized every known detail of his career and his voyages, just what impelled him to pursue his dream so doggedly has remained concealed behind a blur of speculation and legend. Why was a humble merchant sailor of little formal learning driven to sacrifice the best years of his life to the launching of so ambitious and farsighted an enterprise?

Straining against the force of twenty-foot waves, the Niña's *helmsman braces his feet against wooden blocks hammered into the deck.*

T here are few historical characters about whom scholarly controversy has raged with such vehemence. The records that survive suggest Columbus was a compulsive social climber and snob, a religious zealot and a prickly character who would knock down and kick any man who stood in his way. He was materialistic, obsessive and a skillful self-promoter capable of sweet-talking his way into the company of kings and queens. Yet he seems to have been an entrancing person to know, a loyal father and a good man to have on your side when the going got tough. The popular image portrayed in statues and stories, conversely, is that of an almost saintly visionary who, as every student knows, "sailed the ocean blue in fourteen hundred and ninety-two."

The facts about his early life are relatively few, and even these can be interpreted in different ways. For example, despite convincing evidence that he was born in Genoa and learned the arts of high-seas navigation in Portugal, entire books have been written to support arguments that he was Greek or Jewish. A secretive man, Columbus

(Above) Dr. Coin describes to his crew the route the new Niña will follow in the summer of 1990.

(Above right) A young crewmember "parcels," or wraps, a rope with canvas to protect it from wear.

himself told only part of a story here, another part there.

After so many centuries, was it conceivable that real flesh and blood could be put on the bones of one of the most researched and written-about figures in history? Could a hard voyage across the Atlantic bring a legendary hero into human focus?

The key to the understanding of Columbus's first voyage is his *Diario,* or daily journal. Although the log survives only as a summary extracted from a copy of the original made by a priest named Bartolomé de las Casas about twenty-five years after Columbus's death, it has long been regarded by historians as a reliable document. Dr. Coin demonstrated, however, that the journal was never analyzed by an expert with sufficient maritime knowledge to identify and make sense of its many nautical inconsistencies. His fresh assessment of this crucial source would ultimately lead to our *Niña* setting her course in 1990 across what was known in the fifteenth century as "the green sea of darkness."

This modern detective story began in 1974, when Luís Coin was the second mate of a bulk carrier pounding across the Atlantic. The voyages of Columbus were the young seaman's hobby. One evening, when studying the *Diario,* he noted it reported that for several days after Columbus's three ships left the Canaries they were struggling against contrary currents. But Coin knew from his experience as a professional mariner that in the waters due west of the Canaries, where Columbus purported to be, the currents invariably traveled from east to west and should therefore have been favorable. As the remark was hardly the kind of error likely to have been made by a copyist, Coin began to wonder whether Columbus had deliberately laid a false trail.

The deeper he investigated, the more Coin unearthed nautical inconsistencies, anomalies and plain contradictions that threw the authenticity of the discoverer's journal into doubt. Somehow

Continued on page 18

(Above) Making mid-ocean repairs to the caravel's sails.
(Below) The Niña at twilight off the African coast.

Columbus's ships had managed to sail long distances on days of calm weather. Land and river birds were seen hundreds of miles from land—not the waifs and strays occasionally encountered in mid-ocean, but whole flocks, day after day. His seamen went swimming when the navigational data implies that the fleet was averaging a speed of five or six knots, yet no sailor in his right mind jumps over the side unless his ship is dead in the water.

Clearly there was something seriously wrong with the one document of so-called unimpeachable veracity on which historians have relied for so long.

Until I met Dr. Coin at the Cadiz nautical school, where he was teaching navigation to the supertanker captains of the future, I, too, had accepted the *Diario* as gospel. One could hardly argue with the reported speech of Columbus himself. From knocking around the globe in a variety of ships and yachts, I knew that a mariner who crammed on sail and dashed toward an unknown lee shore in the middle of the night might as well be committing suicide, yet I accepted a description of such an event from Columbus. After all, even the most eminent of scholars had failed to challenge this and similar pieces of nautical nonsense recorded by Columbus in his log.

The American historian Samuel Eliot Morison, who sailed the route set out in the journal and whose biography of Columbus won a Pulitzer Prize in 1942, grandly glossed over many of the awkward points. For example, when Columbus wrote that he was sailing between islands lying unseen to the north and south of him, Morison reasoned that these must have been mythical islands that were then thought to lie in the middle of the Atlantic. But how could imaginary lands have shaped waves and clouds in a way that would lead a mariner as experienced as Columbus to make the observation in the first place?

Coin's analysis of the logbook from the viewpoint of a professional mariner convinced him that Columbus had seeded his diary with a trail of misinformation and had sailed a route quite different from that which historians generally accept. But this was only the beginning. His line of inquiry led not only to new data and new interpretations of archival information, but also to inescapable conclusions that, if correct, would stand Columbus scholarship on its head. The most famous discoverer in history, it seemed, had been guided on his voyage by a secret map. Christopher Columbus knew all along exactly where he was going and what he would find, because somebody had been there ahead of him.

To make time for research, Coin left the sea and took a job as a lecturer in navigation and maritime history at the nautical college that is now part of the University of Cadiz.

The idea that Columbus had a map had been common gossip during his own lifetime, but most historians have either dismissed it or been unable to substantiate it. But Coin, through his fresh approach, could now explain how such a map originated, how it could have got into Columbus's hands and why neither Columbus nor the king and queen of Spain could ever mention it. Coin's case, although circumstantial, was overwhelmingly convincing.

The flag of Isabella's unified kingdom flies from the mainmast, displaying in its quarters the lion of Léon and the castle of Castile.

Crewmembers hoist the two-ton weight of the mainsail and mainyard.

Moreover, the probability of a secret map helped to clear up many of the enigmas that have baffled historians for centuries. Believable explanations emerged for why a humble merchant sailor of little formal learning would so doggedly pursue royal backing for eight long years despite repeated rebuffs, why Queen Isabella abruptly changed her mind and decided to back him, how Columbus knew at the outset of his first voyage that he would find land (as he did) after sailing about 750 leagues and how he also predicted his landfall so precisely at the island of Dominica on his second voyage even though he had passed nowhere near it on his first.

After fifteen years of intensive study, Dr. Coin's ideas were compiled into a weighty thesis. In November 1989 he defended it against eight of Spain's most eminent historians, and the university awarded him a doctorate. These findings not only underpin much of the story told in this book but furnished the historical framework for our voyage. We were sailing to demonstrate, in a practical way, that there are logical explanations for the inconsistencies in the *Diario* of Columbus—explanations that shed a whole new light on the most important sea voyage ever made.

Were Columbus standing on the deck of our new *Niña*, his white hair blowing in the breeze, he would see the same seas spinning in white curls along the hull and feel the same lurch as the waves racing up astern shouldered the caravel toward the blue sky. He would smell the same tangy garlic wafting from the stewpot. And he would hear the same song of a ship hurrying into the unknown: the ropes creaking like cane furniture, the mast grinding its teeth, the bow wave hissing softly on either side.

Four hours on watch, eight off—our crew was falling into the universal routine of passage-making under sail. Some worked on ropes with twine and marlinespike or tossed seawater over the sunbaked decks to prevent the planks from shrinking in the heat. Others took turns as navigator, steersman or lookout, while more slept hugger-mugger in the hold like seals on a beach. On the poop, under the eye of our captain, the helmsman leaned on the tiller to keep the caravel on course. But we were not heading due west from the Canaries as Columbus had reported in his journal and as virtually all modern historians believe. Following the route Dr. Coin had reconstructed from the available nautical clues and navigational data, the course of our *Niña* was nearly south.

And with every mile, as flying fish flickered ahead of our bow on filmy wings, there was a strong sense that by sailing in the wake of his three ships, we were rewriting the story of how Christopher Columbus discovered the Americas.

A moody sixteenth-century portrait of Columbus.

Columbus as medieval knight-errant.

Columbus as an Elizabethan seadog.

A 1671 engraving copied from a portrait by Montanus.

This eighteenth-century painting shows Columbus as clean-shaven and white-haired.

Attributed to Ghirlandaio, this sixteenth-century painting is more likely to be a representative portrait.

IMAGES OF COLUMBUS

What did Columbus look like? No portrait of Columbus was ever painted from life. But each century has depicted Columbus to suit its own vision of the explorer, as the many portraits (opposite, left) reveal.

(Left) A Victorian Columbus at home in his study, planning the discovery of the New World. (Above) A stylized Columbus for the twentieth century, shown on a Spanish pinball machine. (Below) This plaster impression of a German coin may well be the only depiction of Columbus done during his lifetime.

2 GENOA THE SHAMELESS

The Cradle of
Christopher Columbus

Christopher Columbus grew up with the clash of hard steel in his ears. The streets of Genoa hummed with war. Enemy galleys frequently attacked the port, and foreign armies besieged the city walls. Feuding nobles attacked one anothers' mansions; riots and brawls spilled along the dark alleys. Political violence was the norm: Columbus's father's mentor was stoned to death by neighbors from their rooftops.

Such a childhood would have made Columbus street-smart and resilient. It would have taught him to look after himself and to watch his mouth. In the tumult of fifteenth-century Genoa, there was no other way to survive.

The maritime republic of Genoa was one of the more prosperous of some twenty-five principalities, states and kingdoms that centuries later joined to create modern Italy. Hardly one-fifth as large as any comparable medieval walled city, it was squeezed along the steep shoreline of what is now the Italian Riviera. Genoa boasted few grand buildings, and its gloomy streets were so narrow that a knight riding through them on horseback had to turn in his toes.

The city's clenched mass of slate rooftops, spiked with the battlemented watchtowers of fortified mansions and the domes of Romanesque churches, rose steeply upward in a maze of narrow alleys and stairways to the Castelletto, a palace that dominated all Genoa. Beyond the zigzag outer walls, green slopes peppered with villas and gardens quickly became flinty scrubland where shepherds guarded their flocks against wolves. Just two trails, fit only for mules, snaked through the mountains that lay only twelve miles inland and effectively insulated the republic from the rest of Europe.

Columbus's parents, Domenico and Susanna, had been born in a mountain region of shepherds and wool dealers. Their everyday lives in Genoa were a round of woolworking, trading, politics

Most historians agree that it was on this narrow, cobbled street, just outside the Soprana Gate, that the Colombo family lived shortly after Cristoforo was born.

and property deals in which Domenico occasionally burned his fingers and ended up in court. In the autumn of 1451 (which is when historians assume Columbus was born) Domenico Colombo had recently been rewarded with a patronage job as warden of the Porta dell'Olivella, a busy gateway on the inland side of the city's inner walls. In the parish church of Santo Stefano the baby was baptized Cristoforo after the patron saint of travelers and the bearer of Christ. The boy was not at all a typically black-haired and olive-complexioned Latin. He had the gray-blue eyes, fair reddish hair, fiery countenance and big-boned frame of a northerner.

The parish of Santo Stefano lay on the city outskirts between the inner and outer walls—a hilly and comparatively open area strung along a creek whose waters were clouded by wool-washing. A few years after Columbus's birth, the nobleman to whom Domenico owed his plum position fell from power, and Domenico lost his official job. So he leased a house from the monks of Santo Stefano and resumed the wool business. Huddled in a dip between taller neighbors, the house had four floors but was hardly twelve feet wide. On the ground floor Domenico set up his wool shop and loom, selling to weavers, dyers and merchants nearby. Like all shops, only iron-barred slits served as windows, so the front door was left open and most business was conducted in the street.

The family grew. Next came Giovanni (who died young), then Bartolomeo, Giacomo and finally a sister, Binachinetta. For children there was no insulation from life's rigors, no special food, clothing or entertainment. Half of all infants died in their first year, and as they grew up they had to look out for themselves. Like any boy in medieval times, Cristoforo was pitched headlong into a rough existence in which the family was the only stable unit in a lawless, unruly and threatening world.

For Genoa in the second half of the fifteenth century, the world was becoming ever more menacing. Over the three centuries of the Crusades, Genoa's fortune had been established by merchants who aided the European knights and won rights to establish trading posts that grew into colonies on the fringes of the Christian world. But with the kingdom of Aragon now controlling not only the east of Spain but also Sardinia, Sicily and the southern half of Italy, and therefore dominating Genoa's entire seaward horizon, Genoese ships had to fight their way out and fight their way home. As well, pinched between France to the west and the Duchy of Milan to the east, the city was invariably under the protection of one and at war with the other.

But the main reason every citizen kept his sword arm strong and his blade sharp was that Genoa was at war with itself. Through the first half of the fifteenth century the city had been convulsed by fourteen revolutions. Its nobility was ranged in two rival camps, the one in power usurping all government functions and appointing the doge, a kind of duke who functioned as mayor, chief magistrate and commander. While the two factions conspired with Aragon, Milan or France for military support, changing sides when it suited, the nobility in general was pitted against the sixty thousand city

The Via San Luca today. In Columbus's time this was Genoa's main street where the city's rich and powerful merchants built their houses.

A procession leaving the Cathedral of San Lorenzo. Columbus's Genoa was a city in which gold and God were given equal due.

dwellers who were outspoken, prickly and quick to riot against unjust decrees.

While a town crier bellowed local news such as births and bankruptcies, rumor was the only true newspaper, and accounts of great events jumped by word of mouth from port to port. Most of Europe was still more deeply medieval than northern Italy and in the process of bloodily shaking off the fetters of the Dark Ages. France, England, Spain and Portugal were emerging as unified national states, their rulers struggling to centralize and consolidate their grip. The numerous local wars bred habits of lawlessness and violence, and because of the dangers of travel, cities were largely self-contained and autonomous, like miniature states. Europe was overwhelmingly an empty, agricultural land with huge impenetrable forests roamed by wild animals, bandits and (it was thought) witches. Doors were barred at nightfall and fear of the dark was universal.

Despite its brigands in the woods, its robber knights, feudal warlords, civil wars and rampaging armies, the Europe at Genoa's back was at least a predictable and familiar world that had the Christian religion in common. But the whole of Christendom was shrinking in the face of a terrifying challenge as the Ottoman Turks (in Christian eyes the most ferocious of all barbarians) flamed out of Asia Minor. The rich trading colonies of Genoa and Venice fell before a galloping cavalry of Asiatic horsemen and nomads who slaughtered, enslaved and moved on. Their mission was to spread the religion of the Prophet of Islam over the whole earth. Those who stood in the way were put to the sword or sawn in half.

Christopher Columbus, raised a fervent Roman Catholic, undoubtedly heard his father and friends speak with horror of the army of infidels thrusting toward Europe. In the 1453 conquest of Constantinople (now Istanbul), the greatest city in Christendom, it was Genoese businessmen who supplied the advancing horde with ships, weapons and food. But now Genoese trade with the east was being gradually strangled. Throughout Columbus's boyhood the Turks continued to advance, sweeping through Greece and sending a shiver through Christian Europe when they reached the banks of the Danube. It is hardly likely that the young Columbus ever heard the Ottoman Turks mentioned without a spit and a curse.

When battles were not raging in the street, Columbus was probably drilled at a tradesmen's school in a few words of basic Latin (the language of law and officialdom) and in rudimentary arithmetic. The Genoese spoke a dialect of Italian mixed with Arabic and Provençal French; later Columbus would pick up bits and pieces of several languages but speak none of them well. As a boy, even if he had had the inclination to study, there was little time because family life centered on work.

Continued on page 28

THE GENOA OF COLUMBUS

1 This sixteenth-century lighthouse has replaced the tower that marked the entry to the harbor in Columbus's time, but the design is similar to the one he would have known. A lighthouse is the heraldic symbol of Genoa, Italy's greatest port.

3 The Palace of San Giorgio (left) and the twelfth-century waterfront arches as they appear today. The palace was the Bank of San Giorgio in Columbus's time and earlier had served as a prison, housing, among others, Marco Polo. The square where the two policemen stand was once water where ships moored to discharge their cargo.

2 A merchant sells fruit in front of the Porta dei Vacca, one of the original gates to the city. In the fifteenth century Genoa's merchants were bidden by law to practice their trades in certain parts of the city. This gate led from the port to the Via San Luca, the main street of Genoa in Columbus's day.

4 The Cathedral of San Lorenzo is a fine example of the alternating black-and-white stone construction typical of many older buildings of Genoa. Originally completed to a Romanesque design, the Cathedral was modified during Columbus's lifetime.

Before raw wool brought down from the hills by mule could be pressed, folded and sold as finished cloth, it needed to be beaten, picked, greased, washed, combed, carded, spun, measured off the warp and woven, burled, shorn while damp, stretched out to dry, teasled and shorn again, then handed over to dyers and returned. This made for a long and backbreaking working day lasting from one hour after sunrise until sunset—more than monotonous and dreary enough to turn a young man's fancies toward bright and high-handed adventure. When work was done and there was time enough to sit out in the street in the cool of the evening and hunt for the body lice that were the bane of medieval existence, Columbus undoubtedly ran across town to see what was happening in the harbor.

Bustling, ornate and picturesque, Genoa's harbor was the city's largest open space and the center of all action, be it mercantile or military. For a boy caked with lanolin from a long and hot day spent toiling with bales of wool, it must have been heaven—the slap of the waves beneath the jetties telling thrilling tales of raids by African corsairs, of crusading knights storming out of Europe to embark for the Holy Land, of battered galleys limping home from battle with hundreds of new prisoners shackled to the oars.

The quays were crowded with vessels of every shape, size and flag, the shoreline heaped with cargo and ships' gear, the cobbles littered with dung, rubble, garbage and flies. Small, open market boats from Corsica, laden with vegetables, melons and cheeses to hawk in the streets, jostled for room with the great carracks, the supertankers of the age, which unloaded the imported grain that was vital to a medieval city's survival. Gilded galleys, splendid to behold with their greyhound lines and brilliant flags, brought slaves and gold from the Barbary Coast of North Africa. They glided snappily into a fort-like enclosure at the head of the harbor, their officers with plugs of garlic in their nostrils to ward off the foul smell of the slaves chained to the oars. Lumbering sailing vessels, worked into the harbor with long oars, brought cargoes from every corner of the known world: iron ore from Elba for the city's weaponsmiths and armorers, salt from Ibiza, sugar and cotton from Cyprus, shipbuilding timber from England or the Baltic, wine from the Aegean. All was trade, and trade was Genoa's blood.

In the Genoa of Columbus's day the one quality that counted was commercial success. *Genuensis ergo mercator* ran the medieval proverb in Latin: a Genoese therefore a trader. What mattered more than nobility of birth, more than inherited wealth or skill with a horse, was profit. The guiding principle of life was irrepressible free enterprise cloaked in holy robes. On the first page of every ledger it was customary to enter the dedication, "In the name of God and profit." Unlike the citizens of Florence and Venice, Genoa's warring people were indifferent to intellectual life. So crass and materialistic was the society that the poet Dante called it "Genoa the shameless." The Genoese character of self-serving avarice was to some extent a conditioning of the cramped environment. The Genoese historian, Paolo Emilio Taviani, one of Columbus's biographers, noted that the city was proud in great things but narrow and petulant in

(Above) The church of Santo Stefano, where the infant Columbus was baptized. In the Santo Stefano parish, Genoa's wool merchants, among them Columbus's father, conducted their business. (Right) An old Genoese street, little changed from Columbus's day.

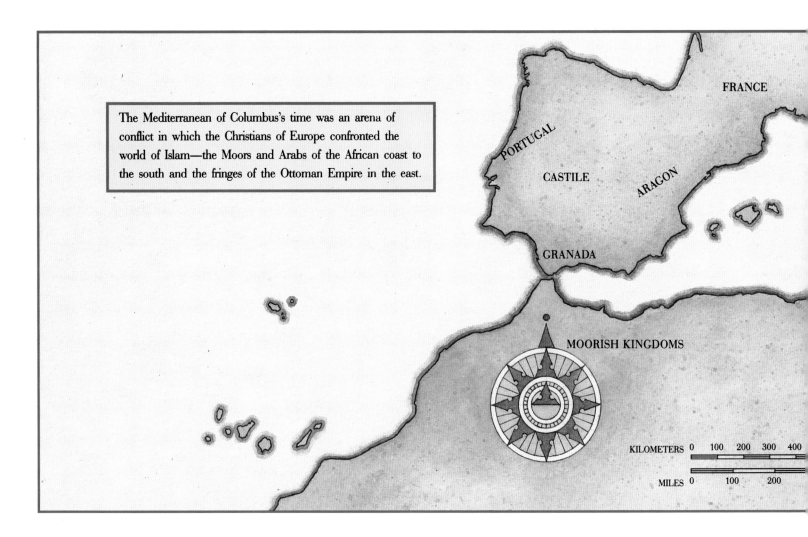

The Mediterranean of Columbus's time was an arena of conflict in which the Christians of Europe confronted the world of Islam—the Moors and Arabs of the African coast to the south and the fringes of the Ottoman Empire in the east.

FRANCE

PORTUGAL

CASTILE

ARAGON

GRANADA

MOORISH KINGDOMS

KILOMETERS 0 100 200 300 400

MILES 0 100 200

the everyday affairs carried out in its dark and steep streets.

The ferocious and often rash individualism that distinguished the Genoese meritocracy in every field must have made its mark on the young Columbus. Unlike the more corporately minded Venetians, Genoese businessmen operated as individuals within networks of families or partners and cultivated secrecy to avoid state interference in their business affairs. Commercial secrets were guarded so jealously that merchants exporting goods refused even to state their destination. It was thought wiser not to place one's *whole* trust in a friend, or even in one's children. It was an environment that taught a man to trust nobody, to stick out for all he could get and to travel light.

With its land production limited to a few olive groves and what herbs could be grown in clay pots, Genoa did have one essential resource in a Europe whose population had been cut in half by plague during the century before: an ample supply of manpower for its ships. Genoa's seamen and merchants patrolled far and wide in search of trade, investment and business opportunities. Genoese vessels had been making regular voyages as far as England and Flanders for a century and a half. Genoese admirals had played a part in setting up and training naval squadrons in Portugal, Castile and even England. Genoese ship pilots had been instrumental in the Portuguese discovery of the Azores, the Madeiras and the Canary Islands in the Atlantic and now were helping Portugal to push down the west coast of Africa. Genoa's seafarers had helped to establish

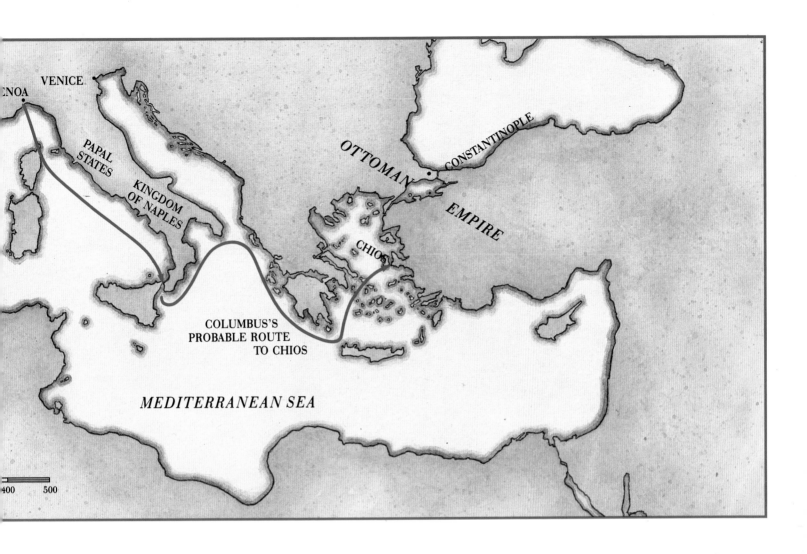

the colonial empire of Aragon, which stretched across the Mediterranean and formed a hostile barrier on Genoa's own horizon, and Genoese merchants had introduced vines to Madeira and sugar plantations to the Algarve on the south coast of Portugal.

Columbus was probably loyal to his father but apparently too independent of mind to want to work for him, so he chose to follow the well-trodden route of generations of young men before and since. At what he himself later termed a "tender" age—about fourteen—Christopher Columbus went to sea.

Of Columbus's early days voyaging the Mediterranean nothing is known, but much can be inferred from the simple fact that in five centuries little has changed in the world of wind and wave. The water was just as hellishly wet for a young apprentice taking his first steps on the road to adventure around 1465 as it was for the young Spanish crew of the replica *Niña* when they trained for our Atlantic voyage in 1990.

Perhaps Columbus first went to sea in a small single-masted boat that crept along the coast to load wool in nearby ports, or collected food from the island of Corsica, which was Genoa's kitchen garden. Later he probably found a berth in one of the carracks (the largest sailing vessels in the known world) that sailed to distant ports. Either way, it would have been a rough apprenticeship. In any ship a boy was the lowest form of life. Seamanship was learned from the bottom up, and that meant washing pots for the cook, hunting for firewood when in port, scrubbing out filthy bilges with vinegar to sweeten

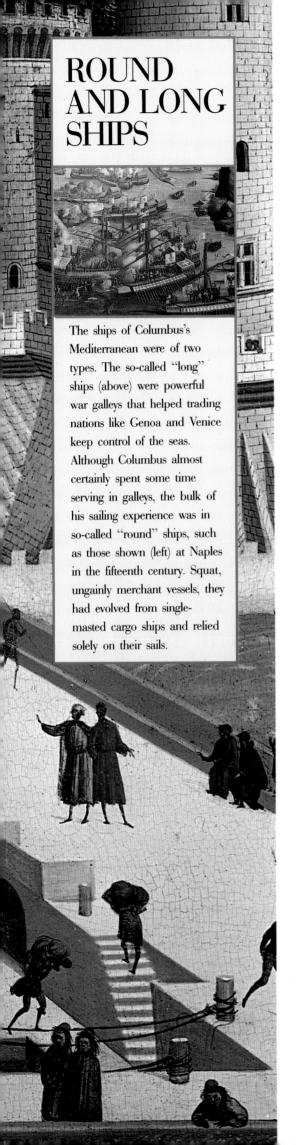

ROUND AND LONG SHIPS

The ships of Columbus's Mediterranean were of two types. The so-called "long" ships (above) were powerful war galleys that helped trading nations like Genoa and Venice keep control of the seas. Although Columbus almost certainly spent some time serving in galleys, the bulk of his sailing experience was in so-called "round" ships, such as those shown (left) at Naples in the fifteenth century. Squat, ungainly merchant vessels, they had evolved from single-masted cargo ships and relied solely on their sails.

them for the next voyage, cleaning and mending clothes, hauling on a rope to lift bales and barrels of cargo into the hold.

Medieval ships were nothing like those tilting cathedrals of spar and canvas, the clippers of the romantic age of sail. They were small, tubby and comparatively poor sailers. Few carried more cargo than a modern street van, and their crews often hawked goods from port to port. Even the largest carrack freighted little more cargo than a couple of modern road trailers.

During blistering calms, Columbus and his shipmates tossed buckets of water over the decks to stop the tarred planks from splitting in the heat. There was no luxury of a hammock to fall into at the end of a long duty, for they had not yet been discovered. Instead each man unrolled a small mat and blanket in some dryish corner of the deck. Waterproof clothing did not exist, so the best a sailor could do to stay dry and warm was to grow an extra skin.

Although the sea was callous, any ship in which one sweats blood becomes a thing of beauty. As Columbus mastered the seaman's craft he absorbed the nautical lore and experience that are the basis of a mariner's instinct—his "feel" for the sea.

The Mediterranean of Columbus was a self-contained universe spanning some 2,200 miles from the hot skies of the Holy Land to the Strait of Gibraltar. Voyaging was slow and perilous. When storms tracked off the land, ships could only douse sails and dodge as best they could or race before the wind. A favorable breeze could make the difference between completing a journey in a few days or as many months, and it did not take a lot of bad luck to be stranded in mid-passage until the following season.

Furthermore, all ships had to be ready to fight their way out of trouble. Any adventurer capable of finding a vessel and raising a crew could get an official warrant to wage war on behalf of one of the many states feuding with a neighbor, so piracy could be legalized. It mattered little which flag flew from the masthead or what tribute had been paid. Those who did not clap on sail and flee or failed to put up a sufficiently hot fight were ransomed, sold to the galleys or put to the sword.

It was common for ships to hug the coast where winds were more certain, virtually scrabbling from rock to rock. Besides, it was always reassuring to sail within sight of land in case of an encounter with some corsair bent on plunder. In the last resort a pursued ship was run ashore so passengers and crew could flee on foot. Another reason for scuttling along the coast was that there could be no more certain guide than visible landmarks. In none of the seven principal seas of the Mediterranean did a ship voyage far without some reassuring headland or island heaving into sight. The kind of navigation Columbus learned was akin to the modern sport of orienteering. He steered by compass, estimated speed as he went along and kept a rough tab on his position on a simple chart. Though practical working maps, these "portolan" charts drawn by ship pilots were anything but exact—having neither a grid of latitude and longitude nor any form of scale—but they showed the main coastal features and towns.

THE FALL OF CONSTANTINOPLE

The loss of the beautiful capital of the Greco-Byzantine empire to the Ottoman Turks in 1453, when Christopher Columbus was not yet two years old, was a psychological calamity for the whole of Christian Europe. The Genoese suburb of Pera, enclosed within the walls of Constantinople, was regarded as a nest of traitors by other Christians as its merchants monopolized supplies of grain, caviar and many other goods and gave covert assistance to the advancing army in hopes of receiving future favors. When Constantinople, shown left in an illustration from Bertrandon de la Broquiere's *Voyage d'Outremer*, fell to the Ottoman emperor Mohammed II (above), the Genoese opened the gates of their quarter to the Turks and their colony effectively became a Turkish town. The Galeta Tower (bottom) seen against the backdrop of Süleyman's Mosque, is all that remains in Istanbul today of the old Genoese quarter of the city.

The risks of attack and natural perils were so great that merchants rarely put all their goods in one vessel. Merchants or their agents sailed with their cargo, and once on board they marked off deck spaces proportionate to the volume of their merchandise. Rudimentary cabins were built on these areas at their own expense and these shelters were furnished with beds, crockery and furniture and stocked with a personal supply of food and wine—all the "comfits to set the stomach right," in the words of one fifteenth-century monk who obviously traveled first class.

From his initially low status of deck boy, Columbus certainly rose to able seaman and perhaps higher. Since Genoa was under constant threat of attack from the sea, it is likely that he served some stints in war galleys. Although he was well known and respected as a competent seafarer, there is no evidence that he qualified as a captain of any standing. However, since the distinctions between merchants and sailors were blurred, Columbus probably followed the example of his shipmates and carried his own ditty bag of goods to trade on the side. There seems little doubt that he graduated from his sea-college years a true "merchant sailor."

Through the long and astonishingly calm summers of clear light and vast blue skies, dry and stable air flowed north from the Sahara to cover the Mediterranean Sea. This was the season of navigation, trade and war. After September the desert air retreated, great depressions swirled in from the Atlantic and bitter winds howled off the frozen continent to the north. As the naval and merchant fleets retired into shelter for the winter, sailors went home to farm or work in other trades. At first Columbus returned each winter to the house in Santo Stefano and the work of a wool merchant's son. After 1473 when his mother died it seems likely that he spent his winters in the small port of Savona twenty miles from Genoa, where his father rented a tavern.

The first of Columbus's voyages that we know anything about was made either in 1474 or the following year, when he sailed to the eastern limit of the Mediterranean into the waters prowled by the Ottoman Turks. After their conquest of Constantinople the Turks had exchanged their steeds for sails and swept through the islands of the Aegean. They were ruthless conquerors. When one besieged garrison held out by taking refuge in a church, the Turks calmly bricked up the doors and windows and left them to rot. So far the Genoese trading colonies had bought their way out of trouble with lavish payments to Sultan Mohammed, but now a fleet of Turkish galleys was reported to be massing for an assault on Chios.

Like a medieval Singapore, this Aegean island only five miles from the Turkish mainland was still a vital eastern trading post. The Genoese merchants of Chios sent desperate pleas for men and weapons to defend them, but these went unheeded in strife-torn Genoa until at last a group of merchants independently organized a small convoy to go to the island's relief. In one of the five ships, probably as a seaman aboard the *Roxanna* (which was outfitted in Savona), sailed Christopher Columbus.

After a voyage of three to five weeks, the convoy arrived in
Continued on page 38

CHIOS.

Traces of the old town of Chios, shown above in a sixteenth-century print that closely resembles the island Columbus knew, can still be seen today.

[1] A woman makes her way through an arch in the town's great walls.

[2] Remnants of the old sea walls built to defend Chios from attack.

[3] The ruins of the windmills still stand on the shore of the harbor.

CHIOS AND THE MASTIC TRADE

Mastic resin was the medieval equivalent of chewing gum. It was a popular trade item with the Turks, as it found a ready market as a breath freshener among the women of the harems. On the southern part of Chios mastic gum is still harvested three times yearly for use in the making of toothpaste.

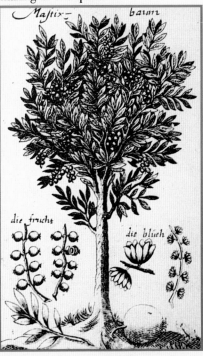

(Left) Mastic gum dripping from a cut made in a lentisk shrub. (Right) The lentisk shrub portrayed in an old print. Though common throughout the Mediterranean, this shrub produces mastic only on Chios.

Built in 1450 by wealthy Genoese traders, this villa on a Chios estate shows the influence of that city in its use of alternating colored stone, here substituting beige and red for Genoa's black and white.

Chios to a mixed welcome. Though terrified at the prospect of invasion by the Turks, the comfortable Genoese colonists complained bitterly at the rowdy behavior of the mercenaries: "They quarrel, steal by day and night and pay too much attention to the Greek ladies," one of them wrote. Soon afterward, when the intelligence reports were proved wrong and the Turkish galleys headed for a different island, the reinforcements were rounded up and sent home.

During his few weeks on the island we can imagine Columbus walking the ramparts of the *kastro* and staring across the strait at the dusty hills veiled in haze, his first sight of the lands of continental Asia stretching away beyond the sunrise. What adventurous spirit would not be inspired by its romantic promise of treasure, mystery and access to the splendors of the East? But to Christians the way was closed. Only the most daring travelers, in disguise and at great risk, could penetrate the Muslim blockade that had interrupted Europe's valuable and important trade with the Orient. If Christians could no longer reach the fabulous Orient by the desert roads, then another way would have to be found. But where?

Columbus arrived home to find the whole of northern Italy up in arms and Genoa in full revolt. The voyage to Chios seems to have sharpened his appetite for broader horizons, for when a group of merchants assembled another convoy, this one bound for Lisbon, England and Flanders, Columbus shouldered his small chest of belongings and signed on, probably as a seaman in a Flemish ship called *Bechalla*. With Genoa still in upheaval, the convoy sailed from the nearby port of Noli on May 31, 1476. Having confronted the suspicious face of Islam at the eastern end of the accessible world, the young merchant sailor now headed west.

At first all went well as the five ships crossed the Balearic Sea before passing through the Strait of Gibraltar into the Atlantic. But on August 13, just as the fleet had reached the bold headland of Cape St. Vincent, Europe's southwesterly extremity, there was a fearful shout of sails in sight. On the horizon was a war fleet of thirteen French and Portuguese ships. Strictly speaking, the French had no argument with Genoa, but they were at war with the Flemish, excuse enough for the large squadron to fall upon the *Bechalla* (which flew the flag of Flanders) and her small convoy.

The battle raged for the best part of a day. Ships were not yet the floating fortresses they would become within a few decades, and although firearms were widely used, the thundering broadside had not been invented, so a sea fight was still an intensely personal struggle. As a ship came alongside and grappled the enemy, sailors swarmed over the rail with as much noise as they could muster and fought hand-to-hand with sword, ax, halberd—even fingers and thumbs. By nightfall three of the Genoese convoy were sunk along with four of the French attackers, scores of men were dead or wounded and the *Bechalla* was crippled. As the ship sank or caught fire beneath him, Columbus jumped. Slightly wounded, he found himself adrift in the open Atlantic with nothing but an oar for support.

From the port of Noli (right), just west of Genoa, Columbus departed for Portugal in the spring of 1476, probably on board the Flemish merchantman Bechalla.
(Above) As this period illustration graphically shows, a medieval sea battle was a hand-to-hand struggle.

The port of Lisbon, where Columbus arrived in 1476, was the bustling headquarters of Atlantic and African exploration. This woodcut, though made in 1561, shows a city little different from the one where Columbus made his home for nearly a decade.

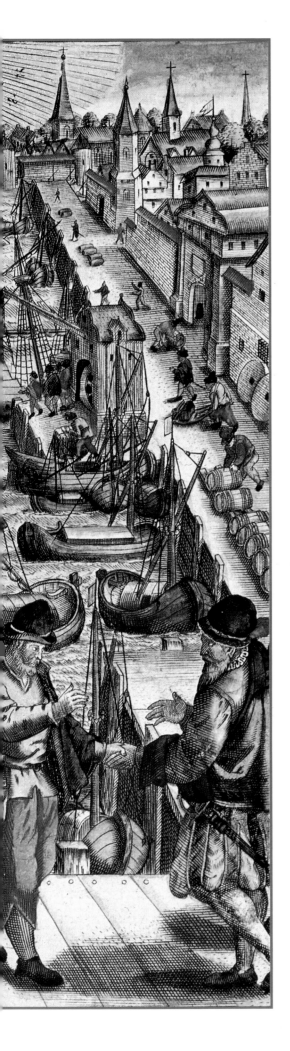

3 THE OCEAN SEA

Columbus in the Nursery of Navigation

The rugged cliffs seemed to fill half the sky. One headland was Cape St. Vincent, Europe's last paving stone to which sailors dipped their flags as they passed. To the south loomed the headland of Sagres, a slab of bare rock with seas bursting around its prow as if it were some mighty ship steaming out into the Atlantic. As Columbus paddled toward the shore, close to exhaustion, he heard the boom of breakers exploding in the overhangs beneath the splintered cliffs, saw the fearsome bursts of spray and kicked for dear life in the direction of a beach. Then, chilled to the bone after hours in the water, his eyes raw with salt and his limbs drooping, he rode the ponderous swells that thundered shoreward until his feet touched sand.

It was a different world facing a very different ocean that Columbus now entered, but he could only have been dimly aware of this as he gave thanks to God for his deliverance. Probably he was dried out and fed by peasant farmers or sardine fishermen who had watched the sea battle from the cliffs. Then he found his way to the nearby fishing port of Lagos and from there to the capital.

Lisbon, with its forty thousand inhabitants, was about two-thirds the size of Genoa. Superficially the city resembled Columbus's home town in the way its maze of tall, red-roofed houses spilled down from the hills to a busy seafront of pilings and debris. The culture of Latin Christianity was also similar, with the same Roman Catholic religion and an equally fervent worship of the Madonna. The Castilian tongue spoken by the upper classes was easy for a Genoese to pick up because it had the same roots as Italian. And, like many an emerging nation in modern times, Portugal relied on a cadre of foreign advisers and investors. Its financiers were mainly bankers from Florence, while its technical experts were Genoese.

As Genoa lost ground in the east to the Ottoman Turks, many

(Left) A lone swimmer walks out of the waves on the white beaches beneath the cliffs of Cape St. Vincent where Columbus was washed ashore in 1476.
(Above) A lighthouse now marks the promontory of Cape St. Vincent in Portugal, known as "the last paving stone of Europe."

of the city's entrepeneurs and nautical experts had migrated west to Lisbon. They married local women and built tall, austere houses in a labyrinth of narrow lanes below the hilltop fortress. One of the foreign experts, working in Lisbon as a cartographer, was Columbus's own younger brother Bartolomeo. It was he, perhaps, who smoothed the shipwrecked sailor's arrival in the city and introduced him to friends and contacts. In short, to this Genoese seafarer arriving in the small but lively little capital in the summer of 1476, Lisbon would have seemed remarkably unforeign.

But if Lisbon had many things in common with Genoa, the differences were far more significant. Instead of the sunny Mediterranean of tideless blue water and serene summers, the seaboard that stretched far to the north was swept by tidal streams, littered with uncharted muddy shoals and frequently lashed by rain, pounded by storms or embalmed in fog. In contrast to the sunny and mountainous Mediterranean, Atlantic Europe was a world of meadow, forest, wide, navigable rivers and murky but immensely rich, cold green seas. And to Portuguese mariners it was this "Ocean Sea" that beckoned. They were conscious of sailing only the narrow margins of an ocean that was vast and not yet understood. What lay beyond the western horizon whence the storms came and the sun departed was unknown, but where there was mystery lay also opportunity.

Almost nothing is documented about the decisive years Columbus spent in Portugal, for all archives were lost in the calamitous earthquake of 1755. But even if the chronology is speculative, there can be no doubt that it was in Portuguese vessels voyaging along the fringes of the Ocean Sea that Columbus improved his education and acquired the insights and knowledge that would make him a skillful high-seas mariner.

Portugal's economy was primitive, with no industry and nothing to sell but cork, salt and fish. Yet the Portuguese had exploited with extraordinary skill and foresight their geographic position on the streetcorner of Europe to embark on a program of maritime expansion unequaled since the days of the Vikings. Hardly one man in fifty was involved in seafaring of any sort, a far smaller proportion than most other coastal countries, yet Portugal had succeeded in carving out for itself a trading empire out of all proportion to its size and resources. For an energetic young castaway with the light of ambition in his eyes, there could have been no better place to wash up.

The little country's powerful grip on the Atlantic was due largely to the inspiration of Prince Henry, known as "the navigator," who had died in 1460. Though he did not sail himself, the reclusive prince held court with cosmographers and astrologers. He supported gentlemen adventurers seeking to win fiefdoms through exploration and conquest and financed expeditions of his own. Their motive was twofold—"For the service of God our Lord and our own advantage."

From a forward base in the Canary Islands, almost eight hundred miles away from the promontory of Sagres and nearly within sight of the African coast, rugged little explorer ships called caravels pushed down the coast of Africa. Initially their aim was to find the

Continued on page 47

Lisbon's cramped streets must have reminded Columbus of Genoa. The capital's old Jewish quarter (below) still looks much like the city the Genoese mariner would have known. (Inset) A view of the harbor today, with the masts and spars of a tall ship rising over Lisbon's rooftops.

Prince Henry, later dubbed the Navigator (left), encouraged Portuguese mariners to begin the process of ocean exploration that ultimately led to the discovery of the Americas.

(Above) Lisbon's monument to the discoverers shows Prince Henry leading a procession of Portugal's great explorers. (Below) Ruins in a bleak landscape are all that remain today at Sagres. Near here, it is thought, Henry once gathered the greatest sailors and scientists of his day to plot Portugal's conquest of the seas.

source of the "river of gold" that flowed by camel caravan across the Sahara to North Africa. After numerous false starts the caravels reached Cape Blanco on the Sahara coast around 1442. But the blighted, baking shore stretching far to the south only confirmed the sailors' worst fears of an equatorial torrid zone where no life could exist.

Desert storms blasted their ships with hot orange grit. A killer surf broke on shoals far out to sea. In calms, when even the hens on board hung their heads and men tormented by dry skin and raging thirst slumped into the narrow strips of shade beneath limp sails, it seemed that every living thing must die. For 1,400 miles the Sahara coast was flat, featureless and hostile. Sun-baked sailors feared that the pitch would boil in the deckseams, iron fastenings would mysteriously be drawn from the hull planks and the flesh would spit-roast on their bones.

Imagine their enormous surprise when, rounding Cape Verde (the green cape) in Senegal in 1445, they came to fertile, tree-shaded riverbanks populated not by wiry and windburned nomads but a handsome, muscular people with ebony skins. The Christian world was astonished at the discovery of blacks in a lush and fruitful habitat of year-round flowers, pleasant thatched huts and bizarre animals such as the great hippos that bathed in the swamps on what the Portuguese called the Guinea Coast (now Senegal, Gambia and other West African countries). When Henry the Navigator died, he left as his legacy a new sea route stretching to Sierra Leone. But the plucky

JAN MAYEN ISLAND

GREENLAND

(DISPUTED)

ARCTIC CIRCLE

ICELAND

NORWAY

BRISTOL

GALWAY

SOUTHAMPTON

LISBON

Though savage, Mediterranean storms were nothing compared to those in the North Atlantic (below), where Columbus sailed in the winter of 1476-77. The map (above) shows Columbus's probable route to Southampton, Bristol and—although this is disputed by some historians—Iceland.

caravels pushed on. Swinging around the bulge of Africa they mapped and tapped the Grain Coast (named for the grainy pepper that found a ready market), now Liberia, the Gold Coast (Ghana), where Ashanti natives panned gold from rich alluvial deposits, and the Slave Coast (Benin). Soon a lucrative trade in gold and slaves was established between Portugal and Africa.

Through this long process of piecemeal discovery, mariners faced a tricky problem. The outward passage to Guinea was an easy sail with following winds to waft them comfortably southward, but the homeward trip into the teeth of the wind was a different matter. For beating into the wind the caravel was the finest vessel afloat, but returning was dishearteningly slow and very hard work. By trial and error, mariners found it preferable to stand boldly out to sea from Cape Verde, driving to the northwest with the wind on the beam for at least 100 leagues (about 320 sea miles) or until they caught the westerly winds that would drive them home. In the course of this wide sweep out into the ocean, seafarers not only gained confidence from being out of sight of land for long periods but also opened up a whole new zone of navigation. New islands, some perhaps previously known to the Phoenicians but long since forgotten, were found by chance and developed into far-flung colonial outposts rimming Portugal's Atlantic "lake"—the Azores, the Madeiras and the Cape Verde Islands.

By the time Columbus landed in Lisbon, relatively long passages by open sea were routine. The island colonies were being developed, though life there was tough and a medieval equivalent of gunslingers' law prevailed. The exploring caravels had ventured as far south as the coast of Fernando Po, and it was confidently predicted that the coast would continue trending eastward and that they would soon break out into the Indian Ocean and open a new direct sea route to the fabulous riches of India.

But in the summer of 1476 the discovery business was in a severe recession. No longer did convoys of caravels sail in from Guinea with exotic cargoes and exciting news. The slave market was pleading for stock. Ships grew weed on their bottoms while rocking at anchor. King Alfonso V of Portugal was waging an ill-fated war with Castile, his main rival for the African trade.

If Columbus was intrigued by the career possibilities that Lisbon could offer, it seems to have been some time before he decided to make it his home. First of all he had a living to make. In autumn of 1476, after only a few weeks ashore, he sailed north, probably working as a seaman. Although almost nothing is known about this trip apart from Columbus's own references years later to his ports of call, it was certainly utterly different from anything he had ever experienced.

The first few days out were an easy sail, even if the swells rolling in from the boundless Atlantic were enormous. Then came Cape Finisterre on the northwest corner of Spain. This was the medieval voyager's cape of fear. Beyond, the terrors began.

The Bay of Biscay was a 400-mile passage in open ocean with no landmarks and no possibility of shelter from its notorious storms.

Then came the formidably dangerous Brittany Peninsula, where the low and heather-tufted skerries are often blotted out by fog or rain, and tides race so fiercely that the rocks leave wakes as if they were speedboats. Off its tip lies the island of Ushant—such a deathtrap that when sighted by mariners under sail it was usually too close to avoid. Even in those days Columbus might have heard the old sailors' adage, "See Ushant and die."

Mariners groped along the daunting and uncharted coasts of northern waters by sounding with a weighted line that brought up samples of the sand, shingle or mud on the seabed. For a pilot worth his salt, a sniff of the bottom could be as good as a signpost. One Mediterranean seafarer observed of the lead-and-line method of pilotage: "Of course, you English always look down below, and the Evil One down there helps you, while we look up into the stars, and the Queen of Heaven helps us."

With the first winter gales snapping at his heels, Columbus's ship crossed the stormy Bay of Biscay and probably scudded up the Channel to Southampton, which for two centuries had been the undisputed headquarters of all Italian shipping in English waters. Next it is likely he sailed directly to Bristol, England's Atlantic gateway and most prosperous seaport after London. For a seafarer accustomed to relatively still and stable water, as Columbus was, the spectacle of turbid whirlpools raging in the Bristol Channel—a gorge that was one moment a deep and navigable channel and the next a chasm between steep walls of glistening mud—must have been nothing less than astonishing. At the river mouth, where the tides are the second highest in the world, the sea twice daily rose as much as forty-two feet, and crews had to look lively to tend mooring lines as the water level changed. Perhaps Columbus wondered where these enormous tides came from.

The geographic enigmas of the Atlantic were as much a topic of burning speculation in Bristol as in Lisbon. With their Icelandic trade slumping due to political troubles with Denmark, the Bristol merchants were desperate for new sources of the fish that they traded to the Portuguese for wine. Because mercantile matters were as secret in Bristol as elsewhere, few records were kept of ships that were dispatched on fruitless hunts for virgin fishing grounds and new Atlantic islands with sheltered harbors where fish could be preserved and ships reprovisioned.

It was, however, well known that beyond Iceland lay the bleak shores of Greenland. And the existence of land even farther to the west was an accepted fact, though it was seldom visited. Nearly five centuries had passed since Norse adventurers had first touched on the coasts of Labrador, Newfoundland, Nova Scotia and possibly New England, settling briefly before being driven out by hostile natives. But in the intervening time Icelanders had continued to make occasional voyages there to collect timber. In the hunt for new fishing grounds, those faraway lands were now assuming new significance, and Columbus undoubtedly heard much about them as he haunted the quays, taverns and counting houses of Bristol.

Just as historians have argued endlessly over the birth date and

Bristol at low tide. For a sailor from the tideless Mediterranean, such variations in water level must have seemed amazing.

Fish being dried by the traditional methods—wind and sun—in Iceland. If Columbus did indeed sail to Iceland, it would have been in a Bristol ship trading for dried fish.

ancestry of Columbus and whether he was a merchant or a sailor, whole books have been devoted to the question of whether he sailed as far as Iceland. Later in life he sometimes said he had done so, though at least once he mentioned only England, not Iceland, while boasting of his wide experience. Most historians believe he did venture into polar waters, and this conclusion is supported by the fact that the winter of 1476-77 was particularly mild. Even so, it would have been a hard voyage that must have caused him to wonder why he had forsaken the sunlit seas of his home waters for the gray skies, slippery decks and howling westerlies of the north Atlantic. The waves crashing over the rail were the temperature of melting ice, the air even colder. The rain tasted of salt as he stumbled out into the disheveled wilderness to heave on frozen ropes, the icy wind knifing through his fleecy sheepskin jerkin and woolen cap. In theory, land could be visible for all but a few hours of the voyage, though it may well be hidden for days by sleet or darkness. Though wild and desolate, these northern seas are similar to the Mediterranean in the sense that every gap between the convenient stepping stones of land is comparatively narrow.

With spring approaching and the days rapidly getting longer, Columbus's ship either did some fishing to the north of Iceland or was driven there by storm. Tossing on immense seas, he is said to have sighted the majestic alpine pinnacles of uninhabited Jan Mayen Island, well inside the Arctic Circle, its butterfly outline so indelibly imprinted on his mind that it would later appear with remarkable accuracy on a map drawn mostly from his own navigational knowledge. As no pack ice was encountered, he afterward assumed that if his ship had continued it would have opened an ice-free route to the North Pole.

When Columbus landed back in Lisbon, probably in the summer of 1477, it is likely that his brother Bartolomeo introduced him to the Genoese chart-making fraternity of which he was a member. It was through them that Columbus learned of a top-secret development in high-seas navigation, which had come about as a by-product of Portugal's war with Castile. While Columbus had been sailing in northern waters, an armada of Castilian caravels sweeping down on the Cape Verde Islands had kidnapped Portugal's governor and taken possession of this strategically vital gateway to Guinea. For Portugal it was a catastrophe, because her caravels bound to and from the gold source in Guinea could no longer avoid enemy patrols. But a team of navigational experts at the Portuguese Court had been working on contingency plans since the outbreak of war. Their solution was to avoid the coast and all Castilian-held outposts by forging a new oceanic bypass. It was a desperate solution because no vessel had been known deliberately to voyage beyond sight

Continued on page 54

(Left) Viking influence can be seen in the door of this traditional Icelandic sod farmhouse (below right) of the kind that was common in the fifteenth century. The area of Iceland where it is thought Columbus visited had sent the first explorers to Greenland and, from there, to the North American continent 500 years earlier. These events had been recorded in sagas that were still being repeated in Columbus's time.

of land for nearly three thousand miles, navigating only by compass and stars. The new route seems to have been pioneered by Fernão Telles who, under the ruse of searching for islands beyond the Azores, sailed to and from the goldfield at La Mina in Guinea without touching land. As more and more caravels dared to follow in his wake, the gold once more began to flow.

In the light of the ocean-going experience that Columbus would later demonstrate, it is likely that he made at least one of these voyages, perhaps more, between his return to Lisbon and the end of the war in 1479. But during this period, Columbus seems to have divided his interests between working on trading voyages as a lower-deck seaman and acting as an agent for Italian interests on the island of Madeira, situated in balmy latitudes about a five days' sail southwest of Lisbon. By 1478 some forty or fifty ships were loading sugar there every year. One of them landed Columbus in legal difficulties.

Entrusted with 1,290 ducats (about $75,000) by two Genoese merchants to buy a cargo of sugar in Madeira, Columbus carried out his mission, but was somehow let down or shortchanged. This led to a legal case heard in Genoa on August 25, 1479, where Columbus presented himself as a witness. Surviving documents record only that he stated he was a citizen of Genoa, was twenty-seven years old and had to leave for Lisbon the next morning. There is no evidence that he ever returned to Genoa.

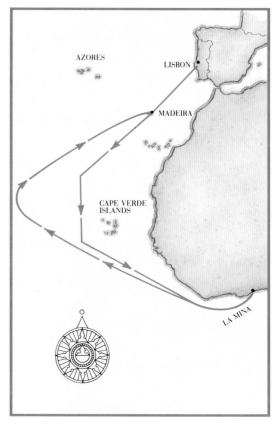

Columbus's probable "high seas" route from Portugal to La Mina in Guinea. In a little under five years, Columbus had sailed from the eastern end of the Mediterranean to the northern and southern ends of the known world.

Navigational intelligence was a thriving little industry at which the secretive and clever Genoese excelled. In those days, when the lie of distant lands was imperfectly understood let alone accurately mapped, all navigational records were state secrets, and ship pilots' reports of their discovery voyages were closely guarded.

The Portuguese state maintained this secrecy by a reign of terror. To betray navigational information was to risk certain death. For example, when a pilot and two sailors ran for Castile intending to offer their services to Portugal's hated rival, they were pursued and captured. The two sailors were killed on the spot, but the pilot was brought back to Lisbon where he was hacked into four pieces for display on each of the north, south, east and west gates of the city walls.

Yet all mariners needed charts for navigation, and not all voyages were official. A mass of information could be tapped in the taverns along the Tagus. One can fancy Columbus and his brother sniffing out useful data from waterfront gossip. The more Columbus learned, the more deeply involved in the business he became.

Columbus more than likely soaked up his working knowledge of the geographic concepts of the day from cartographic experts, and even developed a reasonable hand as a draftsman. His own learning in Genoa had been rudimentary, and it is doubtful that he could do more than read and write, if that, yet he was shrewd enough to recognize the need to improve himself. He schooled himself in the Castilian language, which he wrote for the rest of his life, though with the mistakes typical of a Portuguese. He took up Latin, or improved on the little he knew, and mastered it sufficiently to comprehend scholarly works.

For an untutored seaman this personal renaissance must have been a tough challenge, but it was worth it. One indication of Columbus's increasing comfort in Lisbon society was the adaptation of his name to the local version of Cristovão Colom (or Colomb).

Between trips Columbus took to worshiping in the Convent of the Saints, which stood on the banks of the Tagus handy to both the port and the city. Formerly a home for the wives and daughters of crusaders absent at the Holy Wars, it had become a fashionable boarding school for daughters of the aristocracy, but ordinary people such as seafarers were welcome to attend chapel services. It was there that Christopher Columbus first noticed Felipa Moniz Perestrello.

Living with her mother, who was virtually penniless, Felipa had little to offer beyond her charm and high social rank. Her father was an Italian who had migrated to Portugal, married well and been awarded the hereditary governorship of the small island of Porto Santo, near Madeira. The island never flourished; he had died there some twenty years before, and the governorship had gone to the husband of Felipa's sister.

Columbus, however, could not afford to be fussy. He was a humble, good-looking stranger whose main possession was his high ambition. But this apparently was enough to attract Doña Felipa, and their marriage took place in the convent chapel, probably in the autumn of 1479.

Columbus had moved a step up the ladder. His wife's nobility gave him standing in the community, transforming the itinerant Genoese seafarer into a figure of social substance with an important brother-in-law, the hereditary governor of Porto Santo. A man of noble rank and authority with the run of his own island on the edge of the known world was clearly a relative worth having. Almost at once, Columbus took his wife to Porto Santo to live, and before long, in the little stone church behind the beach, a baby son was baptized Diego.

As the decade of the 1470's came to a close the fortunes of Portugal revived. Although it effectively lost the war on land and surrendered any claim to the throne of Castile, it won advantageous terms at sea. The peace agreement of 1479 gave Castile all rights to the Canary Islands, while Portugal would have exclusive rights to all trade, fishing and navigation to their south. The treaty was reinforced by an order from the Pope in 1481.

Now that the Portuguese had a free hand in Africa, the waterfront of Lisbon hummed once more. The slave market was again filled with Blacks hunted down by raiding parties on the African coast or traded with native chiefs. Gold, ivory and sacks of pepper flooded into the capital, and frontier exploration was suddenly on the go again.

The discovery business was given an extra boost when Prince John succeeded his father, King Alfonso, in August 1481. King John II immediately mounted a systematic effort to extend Portugal's 2,500-mile African coast with the aim of finally finding the sea route to the spiceries of India. When his caravels sailed up the Tagus with news of the latest push into the unknown, their captains, pilots and crews were greeted with excitement and hero worship equal to that accorded the early astronauts. Unlike the modern space program, however, this quest brought immediate benefits in territory and commerce.

As the Guinea trade recovered, producing 2,800 ounces of gold a year, the young king realized that doing business with native canoes in rivers left his caravels dangerously exposed to attack. To protect his monopoly, one of his first acts was to build a fort at La Mina, where the Ashanti gold could be consolidated for shipment and kept under close guard by royal troops. A building was prefabricated in Lisbon and all its stone slabs, tiles, timber and ironwork were loaded into a convoy in which Columbus is thought to have sailed as a deckhand.

T his trip to Africa meant that in little more than five years Christopher Columbus had ventured to the limits of the accessible world. From the ramparts of the *kastro* in Chios he had gazed upon the shores of Asia Minor where the roads to riches were blockaded by infidels. He had encountered the icy remoteness of northern seas, possibly as far as the Arctic, and on the shore of tropical Africa he had glimpsed the Southern Cross low in the heavens. In Bristol he may have speculated with merchants and navigators on the nature of remote islands beyond Greenland. In Lisbon he had learned geography, cartography and navigational techniques and improved his skill in languages.

Above all, his voyages had enabled him to glimpse the continuity of the oceans. Sailing among the islands of Portugal's Atlantic "enterprise zone," he had been instilled with the confidence with which Portuguese mariners made long deepwater passages. His sea trips had given him a feel for the wind, tide and wave machinery of the eastern margin of the great Ocean Sea. The commercial cunning and secretiveness of Columbus's Genoese heritage were now combined with the high-seas expertise and professional mind-set of a Portuguese mariner. In every way, he was ideally prepared for the great adventure that was about to begin—the important task for which, he would come to believe, God had selected him.

A detail from the Cantino map, published in 1502, showing Portuguese holdings in Africa. To return from Africa to Europe, Portuguese mariners had developed the technique of sailing several hundred miles out into the Atlantic where they caught winds for home.

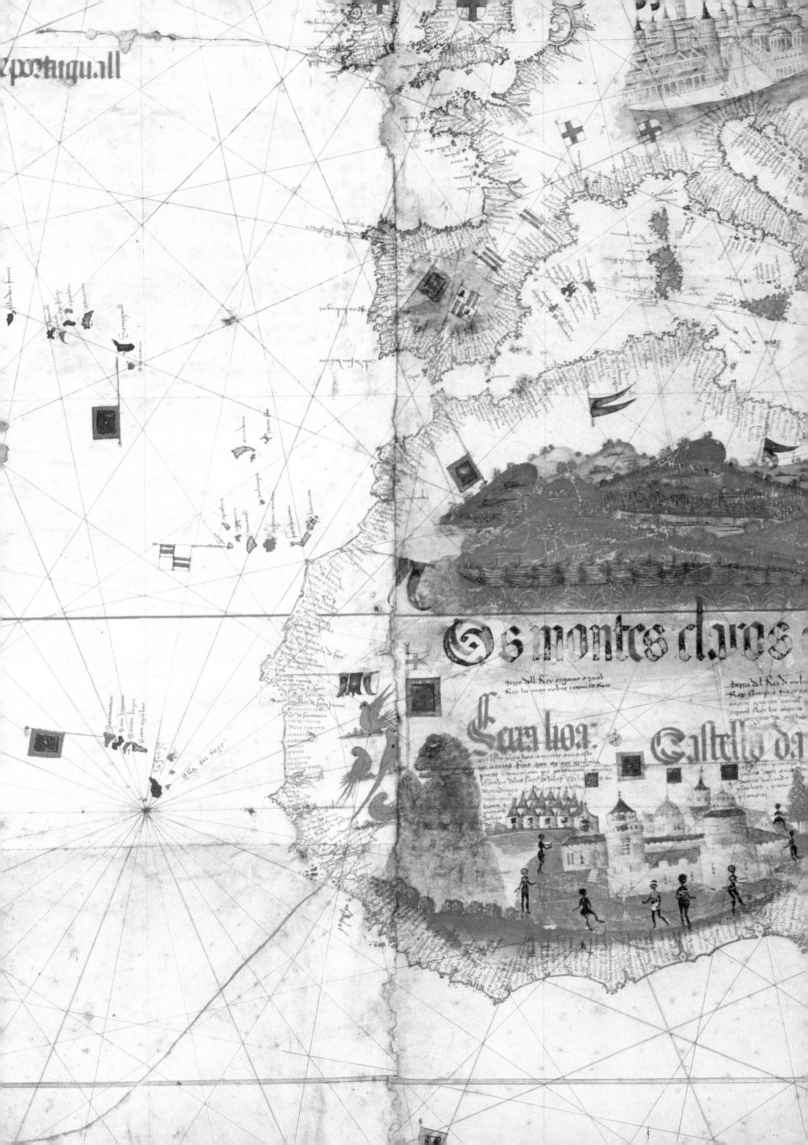

reportugu.all

os montes claros

Saraboa   Castello da

HOW THE VIKINGS SAILED TO AMERICA

There can be little doubt that Norwegian Vikings or "Norsemen" landed in North America, and lived there briefly before being chased off by Indians, at least five centuries before Christopher Columbus set sail. Having found the path, however, they lost it. Their storm-driven voyages in tiny vessels were heroic but led to no permanent knowledge of new horizons and their encounters soon disappeared into folklore. Never did they imagine they had discovered anything important. Wherever it may have been, "Vinland" was practically forgotten and the echoes of it which remained in the sagas handed down orally from one generation to the next gave no hint of a great continent.

The vessels of the Vikings were small, light, pointed at both ends, and sailed very fast across or before the wind, sometimes the fore part of the hull lifting clear of the water like a modern speedboat. Navigators sailed with neither compass nor instruments and probably found latitude by the Pole star, though the skies were often blotted out by rain or fog. Although the Vikings crossed large expanses of wild and open water, the coast was their lifeline. Their voyages from Norway to Iceland and Greenland then onward to Labrador were essentially coastal trips with land seldom out of sight for more than three or four days.

According to the oral traditions which were written down as "sagas" in the fourteenth century, the discovery was made in 986 by Bjarni Herjolfsson, a trader who left Norway to winter with his father in Greenland but was blown off course and came to a low and forested shore. Soon afterwards Leif Erikson, son of Erik who had established the settlement in Greenland, used Bjarni's ship to sail west and came to the glaciers of southern Baffin Island (Helluland). Erikson turned south and followed the forested coast of Labrador (Markland) until he came to the tip of Newfoundland (Vinland) where he spent the winter. Others returned to settle there but were driven out after three winters. Eight turf-walled sod houses and other relics at the site now called L'Anse aux Meadows have been excavated by archaeologists. Evidence suggests that sporadic trips to the Canadian coast continued for at least three centuries. By the time Columbus visited Iceland, however, even the Greenland settlements had long been abandoned.

(Opposite, top left) The reconstructed Viking settlement at L'Anse aux Meadows in Newfoundland and (opposite, top right) the Hvammsfjördur fjord in western Iceland, one of the main inhabited areas at the time Columbus is thought to have sailed there.

(Left) This romantic painting of Leif Erikson shows the fanciful Norsemen of legend while the larger painting (right) of Leif sighting land, is a more accurate depiction of Norse sailors.

4 AN ENTERPRISE IS BORN

To Reach the East by Sailing West?

Porto Santo is a cheerless little island with the defeated air of a sandcastle that has been washed smooth by a wave. Barely ten miles by three, its slumping hills, dry ravines and sand-colored grass seem an ideal setting for an outlaw movie. Many a time Christopher Columbus must have cursed the luck that had allotted this fragment of desert adrift in the ocean to his wife's family.

Porto Santo was not the sinecure he may have imagined; the island made a lean living from selling supplies to passing ships. The status Columbus had craved amounted to little more than kinship by marriage with a governor who lorded it over a handful of gardeners. Not surprisingly, Columbus was frequently absent, earning his living on trading voyages as seaman or deck officer, or perhaps as a commercial agent. With his proven competence at sea and his many Genoese connections, it is conceivable that a merchant sailor like Columbus was easily able to switch roles or combine them as it suited. The nearby island of Madeira was bigger and grander than Porto Santo and growing increasingly prosperous from its sugarfields and vineyards. With vessels calling to load sugar, or putting in for provisions and water on longer passages between Lisbon and Guinea, Madeira was a busy shipping hub and convenient home base for a mariner. It is almost certain that Columbus and his family lived there for a spell in the early 1480's. But Doña Felipa must have missed the social whirl of Lisbon as she nursed her infant son and waited for her husband's return from another lengthy voyage. Some historians think that the family moved back to Lisbon for a time during this period. Regardless, Columbus would have stayed in the capital fairly often and perhaps continued his chart-making activities with his brother Bartolomeo.

It was just before or during the few years he was married to Felipa, by a process that remains a fascinating riddle, that Columbus

The most western beach in Porto Santo where seeds and plants from the New World are washed ashore by the Gulf Stream.

The Columbus house on Porto Santo. Columbus is said to have lived here, with his wife and young son, when not sailing on commercial voyages, or conducting business in Madeira.

somehow got the idea that if he turned the bow of a ship firmly away from the land and continued to sail across the Ocean Sea in the general direction of the sunset he would come to islands and mainlands that lay at the eastern extremity of Asia. By daring to be the first to make such a voyage, he could create his own route to immense wealth, power and glory.

Although the world was known by educated people to be a sphere, nobody had been all the way around it, and in Columbus's time nobody knew how big it was. The uncanny accuracy of the global circumference calculated by philosophers of ancient Greece was yet to be recognized, and the layout of the lands and seas of the planet was still a mystery. Ptolemy's *Geographia*, written twelve centuries earlier, remained the most authoritative textbook available. Although the maps compiled from it were considered state of the art, they were a gross distortion of reality. Ptolemy twisted the tip of Africa to join Asia somewhere near Singapore and made the Indian Ocean an inland sea.

A map of the world as Columbus knew it around 1480 was far different from the one we know today. The whole Mediterranean Sea and Europe's Atlantic shore could be drawn with reasonable accuracy. The lands believed to exist west of Greenland were represented by vague headlands attached to Europe. The west coast of Africa was defined for only a short way south of the equator. The whole of Eurasia, known only from the accounts of early travelers such as Marco Polo, sprawled away into unfathomable distances of forest,

The view west from Porto Santo. Columbus is sometimes depicted standing here, wondering what lay beyond the horizon, across the green sea of darkness.

mountain and desert toward the east; the contours of its coast and the layout of Southeast Asia, though known to Arab voyagers, were a closed book to Europeans.

All that Columbus knew represented scarcely one-quarter of the globe. And there were two significant gaps that most maps filled in with representations of fanciful monsters. The southern hemisphere was thought to be a watery void, characterized by some sort of unexplained environmental chaos where, with the laws of gravity unknown, it was thought the rain must fall upward, and if people existed at all they would have to walk upside down. The other great gap on the map was the Atlantic Ocean.

Not even suspecting the existence of two great continents between Europe and Asia, the prime question for the few geographers who gave it any thought was, how did the two ends of the map join up? That some sort of direct sea route between the west of Europe and the far east of Asia must exist followed naturally from the fact that the world was round. Even the philosopher Aristotle, 1,800 years before, had reasoned that by sailing west one must reach the East "in a few days." But there is a difference between untested theory and action, and what Columbus brought to the question was a determination to act.

But how did he become so convinced that the small ships of his day could reach the East by sailing west? If the story underlying most historians' theories were customized for Hollywood, it would go something like this.

One day, sometime before 1484, Columbus returned to Porto Santo from one of his trips to a very different welcome. As usual there was a mad scramble as the oars of the ship's boat were pulled in, its keel bumped on the sand, and everybody piled out before the next wave rolled in. Then he squelched up the sand to the governor's house near the red-roofed church. But instead of a joyous greeting, he was met with long faces and tears. His wife Doña Felipa was dead. At the age of thirty-two, he was left a widower with a young son to look after.

As he took stock of his life at this crucial stage, a man of Columbus's aspirations would have found little to be happy about. A true son of Genoa, he would rate success and merit in terms of cold cash and personal assets, but what did he have to his name? There is no record of a house or property of significance to call his own, let alone a vessel in which he could trade on his own hook. His commercial ventures had not amounted to much. The prospects for him and his little boy seemed bleak. Here he was, cast away on a godforsaken dead-end outpost with no money, no ship, no home and no wife. By this time, however, Columbus did possess an asset of giant potential. Burning in his brain was his wild idea.

The bereaved seafarer walked alone along the cliffs of the tiny island's western shore, his graying shoulder-length hair streaming in the wind and immense waves rolling in from God knows where to thunder on the rocks far below. Suddenly, the crazy scheme he had been toying with since his early days in Lisbon became a steely resolve. Triggered by the sheer necessity to make a mark for himself, the enterprise in all its magnificent scale blossomed into a full-blown commitment. He would raise ships and crews, hoist sail and steer toward the setting sun!

"It was an intuition," stated Paolo Emilio Taviani. "The intuition became an idea, the idea a plan, the plan an obsession; after his wife's death, it became the only aim of his life." The American biographer Samuel Eliot Morison supports this contention with the comment that Columbus apparently never told anybody how he got his inspiration, and perhaps did not himself remember. In *The Admiral of the Ocean Sea*, Morison wrote, "Any philosopher or scientist who has built his life about one idea would be hard put to say when the first germ of it entered his mind."

Most historians take their cue from the biography of Columbus written by his son Hernándo, which spared no effort in glorifying his visionary powers. According to this version, Columbus filled a mental basket with clues supporting the notion of a navigable Atlantic during his years of voyaging. In Bristol he had seen the dizzying rise and fall of giant tides and wondered where such masses of water disappeared to. On his northern voyage he had felt the weight of damp winds storming out of the west. Like the tides, he decided, there must be some sort of system to the weather. Besides, however confused the legends, there was no doubting the existence of timbered islands far to the west of Greenland. In Guinea, the Portuguese had demolished the belief that the lands beneath the sun were uninhabitable. On lush hillsides in Madeira, flowers and trees grew that were found nowhere else in Europe. Perhaps it was not lost on him that the prevailing winds blowing out of the oceanic spaces to the west were warm and life-giving.

While he was married to Felipa the idea began to grow. In every port of call Columbus sifted more scraps of supporting information from the waterfront buzz that was the medieval equivalent of a daily newspaper. He heard of seamen finding lengths of a cane, unknown to Europeans, floating in the sea, and pieces of wood evidently carved by human hands. In the Irish port of Galway he heard a story of bodies with so-called Oriental features found in a drifting boat. In the Azores he heard a similar story and saw strange pinecones washed up on the beach. Sailors spoke of mysterious islands glimpsed on some far horizon but lost again. Such stories were widely believed because the Atlantic was then supposed to be dotted with islands.

Yet can we believe that a relatively uneducated seafarer of no notable accomplishment was visionary enough to disrupt the mindset of centuries? There's no question Columbus was a man of remarkable drive and persistence, but perhaps there is a more believable explanation for his grand obsession.

A story widely current during Columbus's own lifetime suggests that his inspiration derived from a quite different source. According to this version, either before his marriage or while he and his family lived on Porto Santo, Columbus came into contact with someone who had already been to the Caribbean and returned with detailed navigational information. This story was accepted by

(Above) A view of Madeira today. Traditional accounts of how Columbus was inspired to sail west make much of Madeira's influence on his thinking. The island's forests and plantations are stimulated by warm, westerly winds and many of the strange trees and other plants that grow there, and are found nowhere else in the Old World, started as seeds such as these from the West Indies (right) washed ashore from distant, then-unknown lands. (Below right) The dragoeiro (dragon) tree grows on Madeira and the Canaries but is not found on the European or African mainlands.

Bartolomé de las Casas, the priest who documented the early history of the Indies from personal experience and whose summary of Columbus's logbook is the primary surviving record of the first voyage. In *The History of the Indies* de las Casas wrote: "[It] is what was said and believed amongst us at that time and held certain, namely that this event effectively stirred Christopher Columbus to carry out the enterprise as if it were something that could not be doubted."

It was rumored at the time that Christopher Columbus's information came from the pilot of a ship that had been blown across the Atlantic while on a voyage from Spain or Portugal to England. As it would not be possible for a ship on this route to be carried westward against the prevailing winds, historians have dismissed it as myth. But the story would appear in a wholly different light if the unknown ship were in fact homeward bound from the Guinea coast to Lisbon.

Here is how it might have happened. During the period between 1477 and 1479, Portuguese ships traveling between Lisbon and the Guinea coast were using their secret oceanic bypass to avoid capture by the Spanish. The route required them to sail far to the west of the Cape Verde Islands and into what we know now to be the nursery of tropical storms, or hurricanes. Every summer about eight lethal tempests bred in this zone sweep westward across the Atlantic to hammer the Caribbean and Gulf of Mexico. A caravel trapped in its whirling embrace had no option but to turn west and run before the wind under shortened sail. West and always west it flew, its bow wave piling up like a wall of bricks on either side as it made frightening speeds of up to twenty knots. After days of terror it was left behind by this storm only to be hit by another. This is not unusual. Our own voyage on the replica *Niña* was completed just ahead of two hurricanes that swept into the Caribbean only two days apart.

Perhaps this happened to several ships at different times, all but one being badly damaged and never making it home. This one spent several months exploring the islands and mainland of the Caribbean. Eventually, with its crew stricken by the fevers that later killed many of the first settlers in the islands and its hull timbers riddled with the worms that menace all wooden ships in tropical waters, the caravel set her course back for Madeira.

Somewhere to the west of the island the vessel went down and a handful of diseased and starving men took to the ship's boat. These exhausted survivors managed to reach Porto Santo. There Christopher Columbus, home between voyages and perhaps acting as governor in the absence of his brother-in-law, made the men as comfortable as possible, but in due course they all died. On his deathbed one of these, perhaps a Genoese pilot of Columbus's acquaintance, told of the trinkets he had traded for gold from an unarmed and brown-skinned people on a lush island at the extremity of an archipelago they believed to be part of the Indies. When the pilot died, Columbus quietly took possession of his charts and the heavy pilot book filled with sketches of landmarks, maps of rivers, reefs and anchorages, navigation plots and useful comments on the

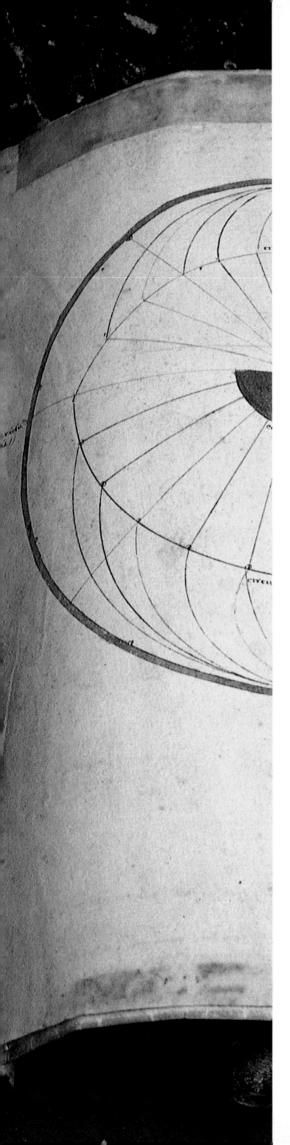

friendliness of natives and the locations of food and water sources.

This story, although it hinges on one stroke of remarkable good fortune, is entirely possible and was widely believed in Columbus's time. As we shall see, it helps to explain many of the inconsistencies in the accepted version of the events leading up to the first voyage and in the record of the voyage itself. The new evidence laid out in the pages that follow makes a powerful circumstantial case that Columbus had some sort of inside information before he set sail. All we know for certain about how he might have obtained this knowledge is that, at some time between about 1478 and 1484, Columbus became so sure he could reach the Indies that he began to marshal arguments to convince King John II of Portugal to back his venture. He could never have revealed that he possessed a map, however, since the king would have immediately claimed it for Portugal and probably had Columbus executed for stealing it.

Had it been simple curiosity that fired Columbus, he would have had little difficulty raising a ship and setting off toward the sunset, but if he intended to control and exploit the trade and colonization of the lands he found, the sponsorship of a sovereign state was essential. A true Genoese, he was already scheming how to ensure maximum profit, status and power for himself and his family.

Before presenting his enterprise to the king of Portugal, however, some awkward geographical questions had to be resolved about the width of the Atlantic. According to the geographical concepts of Ptolemy, the circumference of the globe at the equator was half land and half water. As the land mass of Europe and Asia was thought to span about 180 of the 360 degrees comprising the circumference of the globe, to reach "the Indies" a ship would have to cross about the same span of ocean, or 3,375 of the leagues used by navigators at the time (10,800 nautical miles). Clearly a voyage of such magnitude could not be achieved by the vessels of the day, and this was the reason nobody had attempted it.

But Columbus had concluded, either by divine inspiration or from his secret information, that the distance to the fringes of Asia was only about 750 leagues (2,400 miles), and this was well within the range of a well-provisioned caravel. Now he set out to build a convincing scientific case to support his conviction that the voyage was feasible. Over a period spanning several years, he and his brother pored over the available manuscripts, maps and books coming off the new printing presses in Europe. They seized upon any assertion propping up their case and cast aside any throwing doubt on it, which has led most historians to suppose that Columbus had a fanatical capacity to latch onto one idea. Certainly the case the brothers built was a masterpiece of wishful thinking.

Much of their supporting data was compiled from a compendium of geographic information called *The Image of the World,* in which Cardinal Pierre d'Ailly, the French advocate of Church reform, writing more than fifty years earlier, supported the idea that Asia would be reached by sailing west. In it, they read that the second-century Greek geographer Marinus of Tyre, basing his calculation on the walking speed of a camel, stretched the landmass of Asia hundreds of miles farther east than Ptolemy's estimate. From this, Columbus concluded that the extent of Asia was 225 degrees, which left only 135 degrees of oceanic space between Europe and Asia. Also helpful was Marco Polo's claim to have counted his footsteps all the way from Venice to Peking, thus providing a rough estimate of the distance walked, and his report that some 1,500 miles east of Cathay (China) lay the island of Cipangu (Japan). This left a span of 68 degrees from the Canary Islands, where Columbus planned to begin his voyage. As this was still too far, he arbitrarily reduced it to sixty. But how far was that in miles?

One degree at the equator is now known to be 60 nautical miles, but medieval experts worked on a degree of 56 2/3 miles, which was figured in the ninth century by the Egyptian geographer Al-Farghani. Columbus contrived the view that the Egyptian had scorned his own Arabian mile of 6,481 feet and figured in Italian miles of only 4,847 feet. Columbus might not have realized there was a difference, or he might have deliberately ignored it. Whatever the reason, he serenely applied the Italian mile to the Arab's arithmetic and neatly shrank the world by no less than one-quarter of its proper size. Now he had "scientific" proof that the distance from the Canary Islands to Japan was only 2,400 miles (750 leagues). In fact, the actual distance is 10,600 miles.

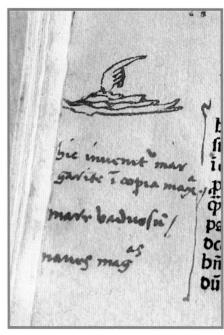

Columbus annotated his books heavily and may have drawn this small pointing hand emerging from the waters to mark a salient point of Marco Polo's Il Millione.

However, Columbus was not alone in believing the voyage was manageable. Through his connections he heard of a letter received by the Portuguese Court from the Florentine cosmographer Paolo Toscanelli. Convinced of the feasibility of the Atlantic route, Toscanelli had even enclosed a map of it. In 1481 or 1482 Columbus corresponded with him directly. Toscanelli's reply was encouraging. "I esteem your noble and grand desire to navigate from the east to the west . . . for the said voyage is not only possible, but is sure and certain and will bring honor," he wrote. This moral support was welcome, but the map, a copy of which Toscanelli sent to Columbus, showed the distance to Asia to be about four thousand miles and depicted many islands in between. Much has been made of this map by some historians, but based as it was on pure fantasy, it could have been of no practical use for navigation.

Columbus could even prop up his solution with data from an unimpeachable source—the Holy Scriptures. If a degree at the equator was 56 2/3 miles, that meant the globe was 20,400 miles around. But according to the Second Book of Esdras, of this circumference the Lord created six parts land and one part water. Thus, on religious authority, the gap between East and West must be 2,900 miles (906 leagues)—even less if measured from the Canaries.

Just how far these arguments were developed during the early 1480's and during Columbus's subsequent years in Spain, and which

The cosmographer Paolo Toscanelli, portrayed here in a Florentine mural, sent Columbus a copy of a "map" illustrating his belief that China could be reached by sailing west from Europe.

parts were conveniently added after his successful voyage, is not known. Nevertheless, before he went to see King John, Columbus had done enough research to feel his enterprise stood on firm scientific and religious foundations. The most difficult barrier he had to surmount remained the psychological one.

Throughout all European history, mariners had voyaged *along* the margins of Europe and more recently Africa. Even though Portuguese ships routinely sailed far out into the Atlantic, they remained mentally attached to the land. As discoverers, the Portuguese were improvers, seldom originators; each voyage simply extended the last. Now Columbus proposed to sever those apron strings, to turn his bow deliberately away from the coast and sail *from* one land *to* another.

It is probable that after the death of his wife, Felipa, Columbus and his son Diego returned to live in Lisbon, where his brother Bartolomeo actively helped him prepare the case he planned to present to the king. In any event, by 1484 Columbus was ready to seek royal sponsorship. He probably obtained an audience through his late wife's connections. He could hardly have timed it worse.

The young and audacious John II, the first king of Portugal to need a bodyguard, was preoccupied with a war of nerves in his own palace. Four years younger than Columbus, John was able, intelligent and ruthless. He had made many enemies in the process of reining in the immense powers of landowning aristocrats, many of them far richer than he. At about the time Columbus was pressing for an audience, the king learned that the queen's brother, the Duke of Viseu, was conspiring against him. Inviting the duke into his private quarters, the king stabbed him dead.

There was another problem. King John deemed himself the spiritual heir of his uncle, Prince Henry the Navigator. As such, he was pressing his caravels to voyage even farther down the coast of Africa toward the long-sought link with Calicut, near the tip of India. With the Ottoman Turks now advancing on the heel of Italy, the need for a direct sea route to the center of the spice trade was more urgent and potentially more lucrative than ever. In 1484 Diego Cão had discovered the mouth of the great Congo River and reported that it was the way to India. With success in sight, why should the Portuguese waste time and effort to reach India by a westerly route?

Even so, the king heard Columbus out and was intrigued by his promise to find not only islands but "mainlands most happy. . . most rich in gold and silver and pearls and precious stones and infinite peoples." He therefore referred the idea to a team of mathematical and navigational specialists that he had assembled to tackle the urgent problem of celestial navigation in the southern hemisphere, where the Pole star that usually guided them could not be seen.

The chronicler João Barros reported that "the King found this Christopher Columbus was very proud and boastful in presenting his talents, and more fanciful and full of imagination than accurate. . .and all [the experts] found Christopher Columbus's words empty for they were based on fantasy. . . ." The skeptical navigators

IOANNES QVARTVS P TVGALIÆ R

King John II of Portugal (left) considered himself the successor to Prince Henry the Navigator and met with Columbus in Lisbon to discuss his ideas for a voyage to the west.
(Above) The royal castle of St. George today dominates the heights of Lisbon.

quickly pointed out that Columbus had his facts wrong. The Atlantic, they said, was too broad for any ship to cross. Columbus, for his part, later commented that although King John "knew more about discoveries than anyone else, God closed his ears and his eyes. . . ."

Nevertheless, King John seems not to have completely discounted the possibility that Columbus was right. He ordered a caravel to be dispatched on a secret expedition to find the western lands Columbus so confidently promised. And the story goes that a ship did depart to the west from the Cape Verde Islands but found nothing. Apparently the captain lacked Columbus's conviction.

When the details of this secret voyage leaked out, Columbus was not only indignant but fearful. The king had shown he was not to be trusted, and there seemed little chance now of launching the project in Portugal. But where could he turn? The most obvious choice was England, where Columbus had several contacts, but that country was caught up in the tumult of the Wars of the Roses. Since at that time France had neither tradition nor interest in navigation and discovery, the next possibility was Castile, whose caravel pilots based in Andalusian ports had experience of the African coast. Sometime toward the end of 1484 or early the following year, Christopher Columbus packed his meager possessions, and with his little son Diego at his side took passage in a coastal vessel bound for the south of Spain.

THE WINDS THAT DROVE COLUMBUS

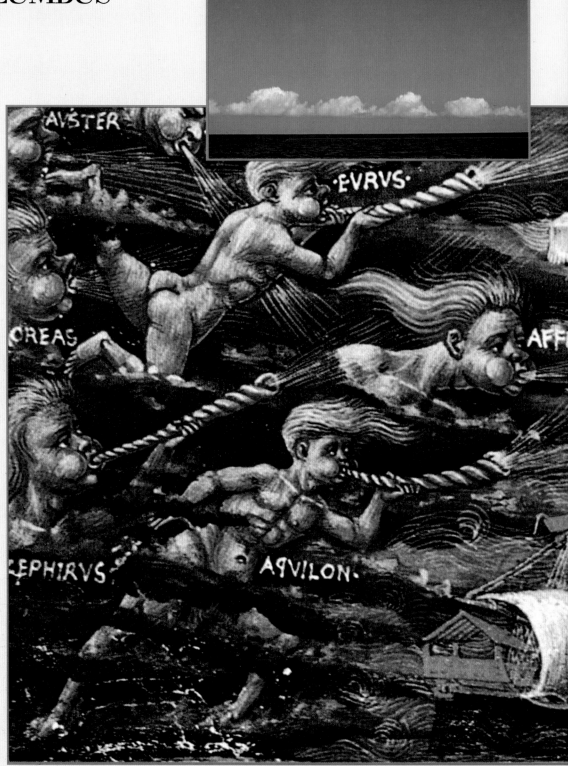

The permanent winds that blow steadily over vast areas of open ocean are a boon to voyagers under sail.

On his outward voyage Columbus would waft westward in the warm trade winds that blow from Africa toward the Caribbean. Homeward bound, he would sail north-eastward and catch the east-moving weather systems moving from North America to Europe. First established by Columbus, this became the usual pattern of all Atlantic voyaging under sail for the next five centuries.

The west-blowing trade winds are interrupted only by the killer storms called hurricanes. Generated over the Sahara in Africa, these revolving storms gather power and ferocity as they cross the Atlantic toward the Caribbean.

It is feasible that a small vessel caught by a hurricane in mid-Atlantic, while bound from Guinea to Portugal, would be swept into the Caribbean. On his second voyage, Columbus found in the West Indies the wreckage of a European ship that might have suffered this fate.

A ship that survived such a storm could easily have spent several months exploring and mapping the Caribbean islands, only to sink on the voyage home with a handful of survivors reaching safety before they died.

Winds move clockwise around the Atlantic (right) while hurricanes born in the atmosphere high above the Sahara storm from east to west along the trade wind belt.
(Above) This illustration from a fifteenth-century text of The Odyssey *shows ships being blown at the mercy of the wind deities.*

To the sailors of Columbus's time the clouds of the trade winds from the Canaries (left) seemed to march like soldiers across the sky. A juniper tree bent double (right) by the trade winds on the island of Hierro.

MADEIRA

SAHARA

CAPE
VERDE
ISLANDS

GUINEA

(Inset) An artist's depiction of the arrival of Columbus and his son Diego at the door of the Franciscan monastery of La Rábida shown (above) today from the banks of the Rio Tinto.

5 THE AGENT OF HEAVEN

Blood, Dust and Public Relations

In six days God made Heaven and the earth and on the seventh, according to the proverb, laid Himself down to rest in Andalusia. In the Andalusia where Christopher Columbus now arrived, God might have rested His horse, but He would have spent the day sharpening His sword. This lush and fruitful region in southern Castile, as big as Ireland, was in tumult. The knight in shining armor, his sword and lance no match for the handguns and artillery that were beginning to make war really dangerous, was fighting his last battle on the field of chivalry. His opponents were the Moors who had swept out of Africa seven centuries before and were now being slowly evicted by the newly united kingdoms of Aragon and Castile.

That autumn of 1484, as his ship shaped up for the bar of Saltés at the mouth of the rivers leading up to the towns of Huelva and Moguer, Columbus saw only a low, scrubby coastline where the great Guadalquivir River debouched into the sea by way of a broad delta of lakes and bogs that was a feared no-man's-land of wolves, boars and birds. Perhaps he pointed out to Diego the spectacle of thousands of flamingos rising like a pink cloud from the marshes. Then, crossing the sandbar and sailing into the Odiel River, he must have appraised with a professional eye, and perhaps with a shiver, the caravels clustered at anchor off Huelva, Moguer and Pálos. In these frontier ports were based the Castilian raiders that preyed on Portuguese ships. Despite the peace between Castile and Portugal, they continued to sail on illegal forays, and feelings still ran high.

Columbus was probably heading for Huelva to lodge Diego with his wife's sister, who lived there. As it was his invariable custom to pray after a voyage, the sight of the bell tower of the Franciscan monastery of La Rábida, on the headland overlooking the river opposite the town, prompted him to land on the muddy foreshore and hike up through the orchard to rap on its ironbound door. Legend has it that the monks who brought food and water for the tired and thirsty little boy fell into conversation with his father, a tall and wind-weathered mariner of dignified bearing. It was a fateful meeting.

At the time, the prior of the monastery was Fray Antonio de Marchena, who took such a keen interest in maritime activities and geography that he was known as the astronomer priest. The friar was evidently captivated by the stranger who talked knowledgeably of the unbounded Atlantic, and so began a lasting friendship that would prove of great importance to Columbus's quest. When the Genoese eventually expounded his project, Fray Antonio was sufficiently impressed to use his influence as the queen's former confessor to introduce Columbus to rich and powerful grandees who might help. The Duke of Medina Sidonia had no time for the wild notions of a Genoese seafarer, but his rival for power and influence, the Duke of Medina Celi, gave Columbus a warm welcome. The duke invited him to live in Puerto de Santa Maria close to the walls of his castle. There, on the Bay of Cadiz, Columbus saw his dream take shape.

The duke was the richest man in Andalusia, with a fleet of his own ships and many business interests. Plainly he was tempted by the persuasive foreigner's vision of a new and lucrative trade route, and as a patron would have been powerful enough to ensure that Columbus's interests were protected. Though he could easily have spared three caravels from his own fleet, the duke even talked of building special ships for Columbus's enterprise. But all hopes collapsed when Medina Celi, prudently informing the rigidly authoritarian Queen Isabella of the project he was backing, was stiffly reminded that exploration was the exclusive prerogative of the Crown. Columbus was summoned to Córdoba, headquarters of her Holy War, for an audience.

Isabella, proclaimed queen of Castile in 1474, had secretly married Ferdinand, the dashing soldier-prince who was heir to the throne of neighboring Aragon. The two crowns were ruled separately but to a common purpose. The young "Catholic Kings" solved the wars of succession in Castile by producing an heir, agreed to peace with Portugal and began to assert their joint monarchy as a supreme and central authority. They ruthlessly brought to an end years of chaos when feuding warlords had devastated the country and brutally preyed on peasants and townspeople. To unite the warring factions of nobility and strengthen their own grip, they mounted a crusade against the last of the Muslims occupying Christian Europe. By 1485 only the mountain kingdom of Granada—a 200-mile-long bastion rimmed by mountains and the Mediterranean coast—remained in Moorish hands. At its heart lay the city of the same name, nestled against the red-walled fortress called the Alhambra. This was the goal of a spirited campaign in which even bishops charged into battle at the head of private armies.

The route from Puerto de Santa Maria to the winter base of Ferdinand and Isabella at Córdoba took Columbus through the great valley of the Guadalquivir. In Moorish hands it had been the granary, wine cellar, olive grove and horse stable of Spain. Now it was

A modern-day Franciscan stands at the door through which Columbus would have entered La Rábida.

Columbus knelt and prayed before this altar in the chapel at La Rábida. Today, the twelfth-century alabaster statue of the Virgin on the altar is surrounded by the crests of the nations of the New World commemorating Columbus's connection with the monastery.

an infinite space of sun and desolation. In the process of reconquest the elaborate irrigation works had been smashed, forests torched, buildings razed and bridges destroyed. So great was the damage of the war and neglect that even the climate had changed. Advancing Castilians found themselves occupying vast tracts of a landscape in which, as the English writer Dr. Samuel Johnson would observe in a later age, if you decided to hang yourself out of desperation at having to live there, it would be hard to find a tree on which to fasten the rope.

As Columbus jogged along on muleback he saw falcons soar over bare white hills dotted with rocky outcrops. Distant mountains floated like crisp blue flames on the horizon. He encountered cattle tended by mounted ranch hands whose wide-brimmed hats and leather chaps—not to mention the slouch in the saddle, the squint and the touchy sense of honor—would travel in more or less original form to Mexico and the Wild West.

The journey cannot have been a pleasant one. Through the last months of 1485 and well into the following year, it rained almost without a break. Trails usually ankle-deep in dust became channels of mud that swallowed carts to their axles. Torrents poured down the hillsides and bullfrogs croaked noisily in the lakes that filled every hollow. The Guadalquivir, deprived of the loving maintenance with which the Moors had kepts its channels clear and deep, overflowed. By the time Columbus struggled in to Córdoba, probably on January 20, 1486, the ancient Roman capital of Iberia was virtually cut off by floods and in danger of being inundated.

In Moorish hands, Córdoba had for three centuries been the largest and most cultivated city in Europe. It was said that after sundown one could walk its streets of mosques, palaces, libraries and bathhouses for ten miles by the light of its lamps. In its midst stood the Mezquita, a majestic mosque of such size that it rivaled Islam's holiest in Mecca. But after the Moorish retreat the city was a melancholic ruin until it was abruptly transformed into a front-line military base. From here, the high sierras rimming the kingdom of Granada were almost in sight, and the infidel capital was only eighty miles distant.

When Columbus arrived, Córdoba was humming with preparation for the summer-long campaign. New Italian lombards, a type of cannon that were the forerunners of field artillery, were being hauled into the city along the flooded trails. Preparations were being made for the impending arrival of the Court.

While Columbus waited, the Court officials seem to have been charmed by the urbane Genoese mariner. In that world of steel, dust and blood one can imagine what a novelty it must have been for the priests, chamberlains and secretaries to hear accounts of ocean voyages and distant lands.

Winter became spring, the sun baked the mud to dust and the hills were clothed in wildflowers and pasture. Meanwhile, the entire chivalry of Spain had been summoned to the field, and more than thirty thousand troops paraded in feudal contingents, the grandees vying with each other in the elegance of their slim, gothic

Continued on page 80

In this room (above) Columbus explained his ambitious scheme for an expedition to the prior of La Rábida, Fray Antonio de Marchena and the Duke of Medina Celi, as depicted in this painting (inset) that hangs at La Rábida.

armor. They were joined by chevaliers of France, yeomen and archers hot from victory in the Battle of Bosworth Field in England, mercenaries from Switzerland and crusaders from Germany, Poland and Ireland.

The Court's return from Salamanca, where it spent the winter, was delayed because Isabella had given birth to her fifth and last child (who would grow up to be Catherine of Aragon, the first of the six wives of Henry VIII of England). When Isabella and Ferdinand at last rode into Córdoba on April 28, they heard favorable reports of the interesting foreigner who was waiting to see them. Within a few days, Columbus was commanded to appear and explain himself.

The first encounter between the royal couple and Christopher Columbus is the stuff from which many a legend has sprung, but only the upshot is known. Neither daunted nor dazzled, Columbus coolly laid out his proposition. There can be little doubt that the queen, her dumpy looks belying a steely resolve, was beguiled, if not by the seafarer's frank and disarming gaze, at least by his promise of wealth, territory and heathens to bring into God's family. Although the sovereigns had no resources to spare for the financing of such a fanciful project, they were nonetheless interested.

The queen instructed Hernándo de Talavera, her all-powerful minister and chief troubleshooter, to assemble a special committee of experts in the fields of geography and cosmography to review Columbus's proposition and report back. De Talavera was the ambassador who had intervened in the tricky question of incorporating the Canary Islands under royal sovereignty and was thus considered the appropriate man to preside. No deadline was set, but the commission would not begin its deliberations until the following fall, after the summer campaign was finished.

In the interim, Columbus conducted a summer crusade of his own, currying favor among the privileged and powerful at Court and forging useful friendships, one of which was with Fray Diego de Deza, the Bishop of Salamanca and tutor to Prince John, the heir to the throne. Grave but amiable, the robust-looking seafarer who had traveled to the ends of the European world must have blown some fresh air into the parochial royal circle with its jealousies, rivalries and ironbound etiquette. By the time Ferdinand and Isabella returned to Córdoba from the successful siege of the fortress of Moclin, Columbus was hopeful that the commission would at last get down to business.

But first the entire Court packed its bags and traveled ponderously over the three hundred miles of high and desolate plains to Salamanca. Arriving there in November, Columbus was helped by his new friend, Fray Diego, who arranged for him to lodge at the Dominican College of St. Stephen where he could talk over his ideas with scholars. In due course, de Talavera assembled the commission of experts. At last, just a year after he had set out for Córdoba from Puerto de Santa Maria, Columbus's hour had come.

Considered in a modern context, the scale of what this man was attempting was breathtaking. An obscure, poor, foreign, self-

(Top) King Ferdinand. (Above) Fray Hernándo de Talavera, Queen Isabella's most trusted minister, was instructed to assemble a committee of experts to examine Columbus's proposal for a voyage to the west.

(Top) Queen Isabella. (Above) Fray Diego de Deza, the bishop of Salamanca and tutor and confessor to the heir to the throne, championed Columbus's cause at court.

taught mariner with neither financial resources nor academic standing was endeavoring to sell to Christianity's most powerful monarchs a highly unorthodox concept. In such circumstances, his nerve was nothing short of amazing.

The inquiry continued spasmodically for weeks, perhaps months. Like an act in a traveling circus it probably became part of the royal caravan as it made its way through one town after another on the long journey back to Córdoba in the spring of 1487. Always, Columbus was alive to the breeze of opinion. From the way the experts challenged his shaky geographical notions and from whispers relayed to him by friends in the inner circle, he knew that the council was unanimously hostile. "In a word, my proposition was a thing of mockery," he wrote later. "All who learned of my plan made merry at my expense."

In Portugal, Columbus had at least operated in a climate of enlightened thought, but here in Spain the subject of geography continued to be contemplated through the stopped-up keyholes of the Dark Ages. Although the details of the inquiry's discussions were never revealed, Columbus gathered from half-heard remarks and contacts that the most learned men in the two kingdoms were tearing into his ideas on theological grounds. They agreed that in his Epistle to the Hebrews, St. Paul (who had carried the word of Christ to Andalusia) compared the heavens to a tent extending over the earth. Therefore, on Biblical authority, it could be nothing other than flat.

Furthermore, any suggestion of human habitation of the Antipodes, the landmass in the opposite hemisphere, was a direct challenge to the veracity of the Bible. Since human beings could not have crossed an intervening ocean, to assert their existence there was to deny that all men were descended from Adam. This brought the devoutly religious Christopher Columbus dangerously close to heresy just as the Spanish Inquisition was beginning to weed out those of uncertain faith; people were already being burned at the stake for less. But these religious objections were probably little more than an unofficial excuse for turning him down. Years later de Talavera, who was a man of vision and tolerance, frankly admitted that he and his colleagues thought Columbus simply could not accomplish what he said he could do.

Although the inquiry never did deliver a formal verdict, eventually Columbus realized it was not in his favor. Still, he did not give up hope. And there were always enough positive hints from the Court to keep his hopes alive. While he waited for a more favorable breeze, he found consolation in the arms of a woman.

Just what it was about Beatriz Enríquez de Harana that took the fancy of Columbus can only be guessed at. She was a young woman of common stock, a twenty-year-old orphan from Biscay who lived with her grandparents. Perhaps his Genoese instincts were awakened as much by her small independent income from a village shop and market gardens as by her charm. As well, Beatriz had one appealing capability that was unusual for the times: she was able to read and write.

Continued on page 84

(Inset) Columbus's first audience with Queen Isabella and King Ferdinand took place in Córdoba's Alcazar Palace (above). Legend has it that the King eventually retired, leaving Columbus and the Queen to talk far into the night.

An equally interesting subject for speculation is what Beatriz saw in the unemployed foreigner nearly old enough to be her father and with a child of his own. She had the pick of thousands of dashing *caballeros*, but she chose him even though marriage was out of the question; the noble ranks Columbus aspired to were not open to persons chained by conjugal links to the common herd. Besides, it was a tolerant age. King Ferdinand himself indulged in a number of adulterous affairs, and the Grand Cardinal of Spain, like many clerics, had an illegitimate family. Yet Christopher Columbus was fond of Beatriz, and after he discarded her his conscience would trouble him until he died.

Despite the commission's failure to back him, Columbus stayed in Córdoba, set up house with Beatriz and at some point began to sell nautical charts. He drew on his limited experience as a chart maker and probably found a small market among mariners based in Seville, Cadiz and Malaga. From charts it was a short step into the business of dealing in the books that were beginning to pour off the newly established printing presses of Europe. But he never became anything more than a small-time dealer in books and almanacs.

One cause for optimism during these years of waiting was the fact that Queen Isabella had directed that Columbus be paid a stipend for travel and living costs. The four payments amounted to 14,000 maravedis over the year—roughly the annual earnings of an ordinary sailor. But after the fall of Malaga, with the end of the war seemingly imminent, Isabella remained noncommittal. And when the Court left Córdoba in the fall of 1487, the payments dried up.

In August 1488, as the king was retreating after a disastrous summer campaign, Beatriz gave birth to a son, Hernándo (Ferdinand in English). By this time Columbus had changed his last name, not to the Castilian form, which was Colom or Colomb, but to the more polished "Colón," which implied that he was descended from Colonus, a Roman consul. For the rest of his life he would be known in Spain as Cristóbal Colón, and his sons used no other last name.

Increasingly frustrated by the dithering in Isabella's Court, Columbus had written to King John II to remind him of the project and renew his bid for support. The Portuguese king was now following a systematic two-pronged strategy to reach India. He sent an ambassador overland to find and cultivate the friendship of Prester John, the mythical Christian ruler of Ethiopia, and he commissioned Bartholomew Dias to push farther down the coast of Africa in an effort to break out into the Ocean of the Indies. Nonetheless, his reply, addressed in warm terms "to Cristóbal Colón our special friend," guaranteed Columbus immunity from arrest for any reason and went on to say:

. . .we beg that your coming may take place without any obstacle to you and we await it and we will be very pleased by it and will consider it with great favor. . . .

The fall of 1488 was miserable. Roofs were blown off houses, rivers flooded and pestilence raged, but Columbus navigated the washed-out trails from Córdoba to Lisbon, was reunited with his

This statue in Granada commemorates the first meeting of the Spanish queen and the Genoese seafarer.

C O L U M B U S

The banners of Ferdinand and Isabella fly from the tower of Calahorra, which guards the Roman bridge leading into Córdoba across the Guadalquivir River.

brother Bartolomeo and arrived just in time to witness the triumphant return of Bartholomew Dias. A storm had driven his caravels far to the south, and when they made land again it was to find they had been carried around the southern tip of Africa. The way to India was open! Columbus and his brother heard Dias explain his voyage league by league to the king. Even in the royal presence Dias camouflaged the truth. To discourage others from sailing there, he reported the cape to lie six hundred miles south of its true position. The king was angry with Dias for turning back, but was delighted with his accomplishments and decreed that this cornerpost of the ocean would be known as the Cape of Good Hope.

The Columbus brothers realized there was now no chance of reviving their luck in Portugal, so they divided their efforts. Bartolomeo would head for England where Henry VII was bringing renewed stability and authority to the throne. Christopher would return to Castile in the hope of catching Isabella's eye at the moment of her victory over the Moors, which now appeared to be only a matter of time.

On the way back, Columbus stayed for a while with Fray Antonio and his other old friends at La Rábida. And it was there, in May 1489, that the queen, perhaps having been advised that Columbus was trying his luck abroad, sent him a grant of 10,000 maravedis and summoned him to Córdoba with a promise of new discussions. There was also a royal warrant ordering towns along his route to furnish food and lodging. But then the king's siege of the fortress of Baza bogged down in early summer floods, and thousands of men were diverted to repair the washed-out roads. For every Christian killed in battle, another six died of disease. The setback diverted Isabella from any thought of overseas exploration. Pledging her gold and jewels for cash to keep the army going, she threw herself into the task of raising the men, supplies and guns her husband desperately needed. By the time Columbus arrived home, she had no time for his project.

As one delay followed another, Columbus seems to have become a well-known and sometimes scoffed-at figure around town—a grave and pious white-haired foreigner, kindly spoken but rather down at heel. Children were said to point to their foreheads as he passed, suggesting the man was a little mad.

The book business allowed him to eke out a living and continue his research. Never systematic, he returned again and again to the same few sources, artfully glossing over anything contradictory, heavily underlining any support and dashing off a few notes in the margins. In corrupt Latin or impure Castilian he jotted some 2,500 notations in various books. Some postils were elementary, even banal, and sound like a cry of frustration—"The Earth is round and spherical. . . .The end of Spain and the beginning of India are not far apart, indeed they are close, and it is known that this sea is navigable in a few days' time with a favoring wind. . . ."

It is puzzling that a man of Columbus's practicality and energy put up with such derision, delay and obstruction over so many years. Most historians have argued that his persistence and abounding self-confidence were in fact major aspects of his genius. But it has to be asked whether a seafarer who lived by rough action would pin so much of his future well-being on an intellectual concept alone. What could account for his mental stamina in the face of prolonged and open scorn from hostile experts in two countries?

His obsession took a new twist one day in the summer of 1489 when two Franciscan friars rode into the royal camp at Baza, where Christopher Columbus was awaiting another royal audience. They had been dispatched by the Sultan of Egypt to warn the Catholic kings that if their campaign against the Moors was not halted, he would put to the sword all Christians in the Holy Land and destroy the Church of the Holy Sepulchre in Jerusalem. This blackmail outraged the ardent Spanish knights and Queen Isabella managed to stall the threat, but it made a deep impression on Columbus. That Christians should arm themselves against Turks and Saracens, free the Holy Land and rebuild the unity of the great family of Christ was a central theme of his fervent religious values going back to his Genoese childhood. Now he made a vow to finance personally a crusading army complete with horses, artillery and ships to rescue the Holy Sepulchre from infidel hands. Such self-assurance from an impoverished dreamer may have prompted a few snickers, but by the end of his reign King Ferdinand was himself promoting similar undertakings. Columbus would say later that he felt himself "the agent chosen by Heaven to accomplish its grand designs." Over his flair for self-promotion and his extraordinary staying power was laid a mantle of nascent fanaticism.

In the spring of 1490 hope glimmered again. The whole Court was in Seville for a season of feasts, jousting, bull-lancing tourneys and torchlight processions to celebrate the marriage by proxy of Ferdinand and Isabella's eldest daughter to the heir of the throne of Portugal. In an expansive mood, the queen ordered the commission of experts to review the enterprise one more time. Columbus lodged in Calle Genoa—now a fashionable shopping street—with his sister-in-law (who had moved there from Huelva) and once again awaited the verdict. But once again the conclusion was unfavorable. According to Bartolomé de las Casas, the priest who summarized Columbus's journal, the word reaching the sovereigns "persuaded them that it did not benefit the authority of their royal persons to support a business based on such flimsy foundations." Meanwhile Columbus's brother Bartolomeo, who had been captured by pirates and later freed, had not yet arrived in England. In his *History of the Indies*, de las Casas noted, "Columbus saw his life was floating past wasted. . .and above all, saw how distrusted were his truth and person."

Yet despite the official rebuff, the queen let it be known that

Continued on page 92

THE ELEGANT LEGACY OF THE MOORS

Seven centuries before Columbus's voyage a great army of tribesmen from North Africa stormed out of what is now Morocco. Known as "Moors" and Muslim by religion, they invaded and wrested control of the entire Iberian Peninsula in just a few years. But it took them centuries to leave.

The long process of reclaiming what is now Spain began in the twelfth century and continued bit by bit until only the mountain kingdom of Granada remained in Moorish hands.

In 1476 the Moorish ruler of Granada refused to pay his usual tributes of gold to the monarchs of Aragon and

Castile. King Ferdinand and Queen Isabella then mounted a joint crusade to throw the Moors out of Spain. This colorful holy war, the last to be fought by armored knights on horseback, ended when Granada surrendered in 1492.

The Moorish occupation of Spain was a harmonious one characterized by intellectual

enlightenment, painstaking husbandry of the land and elaborately decorative architecture.

Córdoba, in the hands of the Moors for four centuries, became the largest and most cultivated city in Europe. Its great Mezquita mosque (below) rivaled Islam's holiest mosque in the city of Mecca.

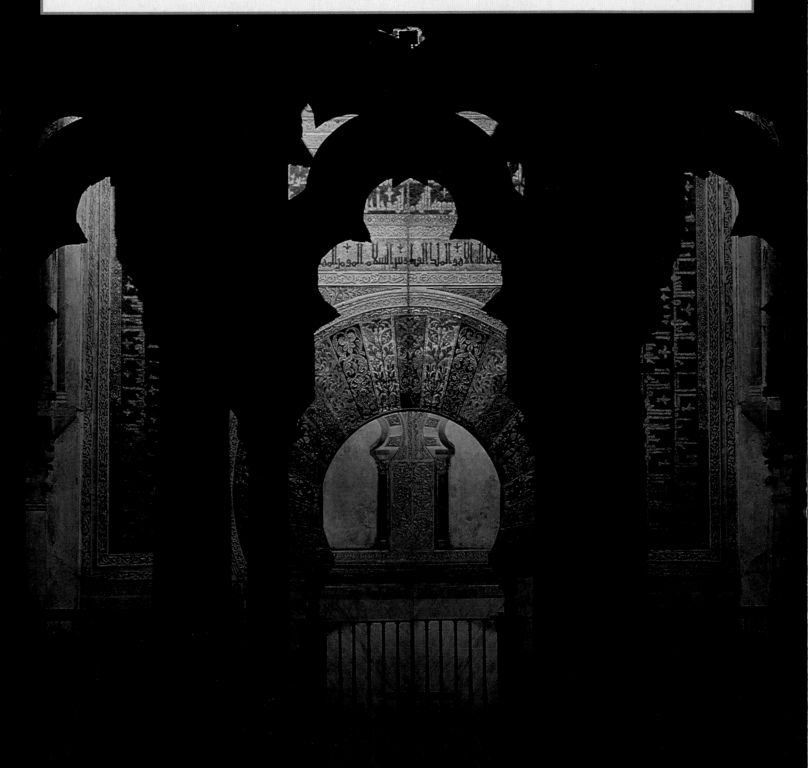

(Left) Moors and Christians in combat at Higueruela, one of many battles fought to wrest southern Spain from its Moorish conquerors.

(Above) Details of intricate Moorish mosaic and tilework from the Alcazar and the Alhambra. Islam forbade the depiction of the human figure, with the result that religious decoration in Islamic countries focused on pattern and embellishment. When Columbus entered Granada with Ferdinand and Isabella after the defeat of the Moors in January of 1492, he would no doubt have been impressed by Moorish artistry.

(Inset) In this nineteenth-century painting King Boabdil of the Moors surrenders to King Ferdinand and Queen Isabella on January 2, 1492, with the Alhambra palace visible in the background. Columbus had been told that when Granada was taken and Spain was at last free of the Moors, the King and Queen would be willing to consider his ideas for an expedition. Columbus accompanied the royal party on its triumphal entry into Granada and toured the Alhambra (above) with its new rulers.

the decision was not yet final. Once the war was won the door would still be open. But when would that be? Infuriatingly, King Ferdinand decided that as Granada was too heavily fortified to be taken by assault, he would adopt a strategy of patience. "By ravaging the country this year," he said, "we will produce scarcity the next." And so, through the war season of 1490, Granada was wreathed in the bonfire smoke of its gardens, orchards and crops as everything on which it depended was put to the torch, while its flocks and herds were driven away in dusty columns by the conquering army.

At last Columbus's patience ran out. It is not hard to imagine the worries that tormented him as he brooded through the long and idle winter. He was in his fortieth year and could count himself fortunate to have so long survived the rigors of fifteenth-century life with his health intact. He would only have to catch his own reflection in a polished blade and see the obsessed expression on a gaunt and aging face to be reminded of the march of time. Though he had renounced so much, his enterprise seemed no nearer to fruition than it had been ten difficult years earlier.

Therefore in the spring of 1491 Columbus turned his back on the war and tramped across the sun-scorched countryside to La Rábida. His intentions are unclear, and history does not relate how he explained his departure to Beatriz. His brother Bartolomeo had finally reached England and put his case to Henry VII, but being rejected had taken his suit to the king of France. It seems likely that Columbus told his old friend Fray Antonio that he intended to join Bartolomeo there. However, fate intervened. Lodging at La Rábida was Fray Juan Pérez (a former confessor to the queen and a man of substantial influence with Isabella) who was dismayed that Castile stood to lose such an enterprise.

Suddenly things began to happen. Pérez lost no time in saddling up and riding to seek an urgent audience with the queen, who had joined the king and his army encamped on the vega before Granada. A messenger immediately galloped back to La Rábida with a summons. Columbus was to return to the Court. A gift of 20,000 maravedis was enclosed so he could provide himself with new clothes, and he was also sent a warrant authorizing the use of a mount, since the war effort proscribed the use of horses and mules.

What can explain this abrupt royal reversal? Why, after years of fobbing him off with half a dozen different excuses, would Queen Isabella send such a handsome gift from her hard-pressed treasury? Why was she suddenly in such a hurry to see him?

The traditional explanation—that with Columbus apparently determined to take his project elsewhere the queen finally saw the light—seems inadequate. He had done so before and never had Isabella been so urgent in her attentions. But what if Columbus had revealed to Fray Juan some piece of evidence he had not previously dared to present to either King John of Portugal or the Spanish commission of inquiry? Perhaps he claimed he had found the information in the papers of his late father-in-law, as his son Hernándo would later imply. This is exactly what some historians have sugggested, proposing that the secret Columbus revealed was Toscanelli's map,

The Columbus Gate at Sante Fé. After Ferdinand and Isabella refused the terms he demanded, Columbus rode through this gate on a mule, heading for France.

stolen from Lisbon, though it could have been of no practical use for navigation. Others have hypothesized that his secret was an explanation of the pattern of oceanic winds he planned to use. But if either were the case, why did he not disclose the information much earlier? No, the secret, if this is what changed the queen's mind, must have been much more convincing.

When Columbus arrived at King Ferdinand's camp, known as Santa Fé (Holy Faith), he was escorted through the maze of trenches and stockades outlying the new stone walls to find himself in a crowded military garrison. A formidable force of cavalry and troops was quartered in tents and sapling huts, while outside mounted lancers patrolled the ravaged plain. And for one last time Columbus waited.

When autumn came with no harvest to replenish Granada's granaries, the Moors capitulated. A treaty was drawn up in November, and six weeks later, on January 6, 1492, Christopher Columbus joined the great procession of prelates, knights and troops that followed the Catholic kings on their triumphant entry into the Alhambra Palace.

The victory was celebrated from St. Peter's in Rome to St. Paul's in London. And at this most glorious moment in Spanish history, her kingdom now united and peaceful, her personal authority never stronger, Isabella did not overlook the now familiar figure of the Genoese merchant-mariner. She gave her consent for "the difficult enterprise" to be reconsidered.

But it was a different Columbus who was now ushered into her presence. Whatever he had told Fray Juan, he clearly now believed his bargaining position was very strong. He no longer pleaded for royal consent but laid down audacious terms. The years of delay had given him ample time to refine his list of demands, and he was prepared to hold out for them at any price.

We can imagine the mounting incredulity with which Queen Isabella listened to Columbus. He set out an astonishing scheme that would effectively turn the Ocean Sea and the islands and mainlands he discovered into something like a principality that he and his heirs would control forever. Although the risks to the Crown were slight, he had the nerve to suggest that he be made an admiral of Castile as well as viceroy and governor of all the lands he found, with control of administration and justice. He wanted one-tenth of all gold and other treasures, one-eighth of the profit on trading ventures and sole rights to arbitrate any mercantile disputes that arose. That a penurious foreigner should be elevated at one stroke to the standing of the most wealthy, powerful and distinguished figures in the known world was inconceivable. The Court thought Columbus mad, and Isabella sent him flatly and finally packing.

The agent of heaven mounted his mule, rode out of the north gate of Santa Fé and took the trail toward Córdoba. Then, in the hamlet of Pinos just four miles to the north, where the trail crossed a gorge by way of an ancient three-arched bridge, Christopher Columbus heard the hoofbeats of the queen's messenger pounding in hot pursuit.

QUEEN ISABELLA: ATHLETE OF CHRIST

When Columbus was presented to Queen Isabella he found himself face to face with a pale, plain and pouty woman of exactly his own age. But the pudding face and graceless figure of the Queen belied her iron will and determined belief that good kingship could protect the weak and humble the proud. Described as a queen of "holy hunger and thirst for justice," she clearly warmed to Columbus but all her attention—not to mention her finances—were involved in winning the war against the last of the Muslims in Spain.

Some stories suggest the Queen fell in love with Columbus. Anything more than some spark of understanding between them is unlikely. While her husband Ferdinand philandered, the prudish and devout Isabella was deeply involved in the short and unhappy lives of her children. Prince John, the heir, was a sickly little boy who died young. Her oldest daughter was widowed after six months of marriage to the heir of Portugal who died in a riding accident. Another daughter, Catherine of Aragon became one of the unlucky wives of Henry VIII of England.

As a young woman,

Isabella of Castile could have married her way to the thrones of England or France but in 1469 she chose Aragon because the union of the two most powerful kingdoms of Spain promised a more lasting political result. Isabella succeeded to her throne in 1474 and Ferdinand to his in 1479. The two kingdoms remained distinct, with separate laws, parliaments and frontiers, but general affairs were transacted under a common seal. The reforms of "the Catholic Kings" put an end to the anarchy of the Spanish nobles and imposed a rigid and effective system of justice. They also established the Inquisition and expelled the Jews from Spain. Although they successfully fought Rome for direct control of the Church, the Pope described the young monarchs as "the athletes of Christ."

Demure but tough, Isabella's whole heart when Columbus met her was in the campaign to drive out the Moors. She pledged the Crown's gold and plate and her personal jewels to raise money, obtained materials and set up forges to construct weapons, and assembled an immense body of workers to construct roads and bridges. She was not loath to don a

breastplate over her brocade gown and ride off to join her husband, giving heart to her troops. Her energy was matched by her imagination and it was this quality which seems to have been most touched by the tall Genoese seafarer with the curiously white hair who haunted the margins of her Court in his quest for royal support.

(Top left) A relief of Ferdinand and Isabella on a wall of the University of Salamanca. (Below) The gate through which Ferdinand and Isabella left their encampment at Sante Fé to enter the Moorish stronghold of Granada. (Right) Isabella's plain looks are attested to in this unusually frank portrait painted during her lifetime.

THE DEADLY WORK OF THE SPANISH INQUISITION

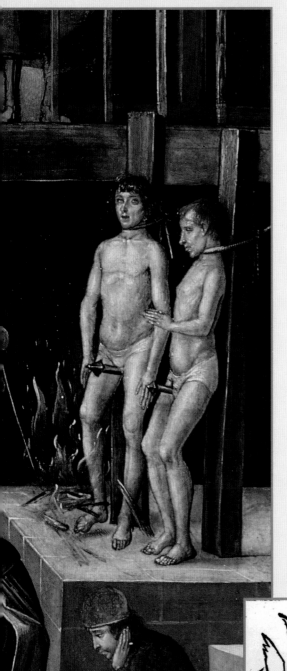

The infamous Inquisition began just before Columbus arrived in Spain. Earlier, Spain had been the model of a multi-racial and multi-religious society. Jews, returned Moors and foreigners were necessary to populate the vast lands reconquered from the Moors and provide commercial skills.

But the Jews were passionately resented because they collected taxes and controlled all finances. To evade harsh measures taken against them, many Jews and Moors professed conversion to Christianity.

The new faith of the so-called "conversos," however, soon came under suspicion as a mockery of Christ. For this reason the Pope was persuaded by Ferdinand and Isabella to allow the establishment of a tribunal to detect and punish false conversions.

Controlled by the monarchs but operated by the church, the Inquisition soon inspired terror and revulsion throughout Europe but not even the Pope could stop it. Denunciations were made in confidence, trials were held in secret and victims had no right to cross-question their accusers. Confessions were extracted under torture and the guilty burned at the stake, their properties shared equally between the accusers, the inquisitors and the Crown.

Many Jews and conversos fled, thus paralyzing Spain's bureaucracy and crippling its mercantile life. Their exodus left business largely in the hands of the Genoese. Had Columbus himself been Jewish, as some historians have alleged, it is inconceivable, in the light of the many enemies he made after his discovery voyage, that he would have escaped the clutches of the Inquisition.

(Left) This late fifteenth-century painting by Pedro Berruguete depicts the burning of heretics condemned by the judges of the Inquisition. (Above) The burning of Jews in Spain. This practice began in Seville in 1481 when six Jews, both men and women, were burned alive.

(Inset) The queen's messenger caught up with Columbus as he was crossing the bridge at Pinos as shown in this painting.
(Above) The Pinos bridge is still in use today, although somewhat changed by the addition of a tower and a coating of whitewash.

6 THE QUEEN'S BLESSING

In the Name of God, Make Sail!

Even as Christopher Columbus packed his saddlebag for the ride to Córdoba, it seems that Luís de Santangel, one of the astute and farsighted friends whom Columbus had cultivated, had heard of Queen Isabella's curt refusal of the mariner's terms and was hurrying to her side. A wealthy lawyer who handled the Court's finances, de Santangel knew better than anybody the monarchy's desperate state of poverty after ten years of war. He was just the man to strip the project of its ecclesiastical and philosophical hocus-pocus and present it in the cold context of an investment opportunity the Crown could ill afford to miss.

At a single stroke Spain might eclipse the decades of patient Portuguese endeavor to reach the Indies. Besides, Spain was overflowing with thousands of spirited young *hidalgos* from the lower gentry seeking chances to quench their thirst for honor now that the Moors had been defeated. More significantly, the risks of backing Columbus were minimal. If he failed, little would be lost but his own head. If he succeeded, his reward would have been well earned.

Even so, Isabella perhaps demurred, where was the money to come from? Her treasury was empty, and the venture capital required was about two million maravedis. (The fable that Isabella pawned her jewels to finance the expedition was invented in the seventeenth century; in fact, her gems had already been mortgaged to buy guns.) But the clever accountant had an answer to the money problems. Two of the three caravels Columbus demanded could be levied on the seaport town of Pálos in lieu of a fine its seamen had incurred for some sort of smuggling offence. As for the third, Columbus himself had said he would invest about 250,000 maravedis raised from a consortium of four Genoese and Florentine merchants in Seville. This left a shortfall of about 1.14 million maravedis, which Luís de

(Inset) In the church of St. George at Pálos on May 23, 1492, the local magistrate read a royal edict ordering the people of the town to supply Columbus with ships and provisions. The distinctive wrought-iron pulpit (above) can still be seen in the church today.

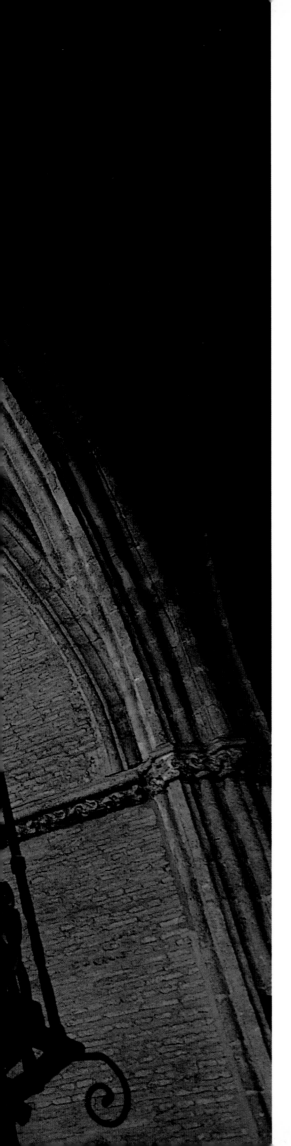

Santangel, in his capacity as treasurer of the organization of police patrols known as the Holy Brotherhood, would advance to the Crown at 14 percent over two years.

The queen was convinced and sent word to Columbus that his terms were accepted. This was the news carried by the messenger who caught up to him on the road to Córdoba. At last he could assemble a fleet of ships and men and issue the order of which he had dreamed for so long—"In the name of God, make sail!"

Where did Columbus think he was going? Historians have made much of the notion that he thought he was sailing to Japan and China, but the contract finally signed by the sovereigns on April 17, 1492, mentions only unspecified islands and mainlands toward the west. If Columbus had read Marco Polo before his departure, would he so naively have entertained the idea that China, with its vast armies, well-established government, religion and vast riches, could be subdued by his puny force of ninety men? The so-called Grand Khan had a bodyguard of twelve thousand men and controlled armies many times larger. Columbus could not seriously have imagined he would become "Governor and Viceroy" of such a place. For whatever reason, he seems to have been quite certain he would discover lands quite different than the highly advanced countries China and Japan were known to be.

Columbus finally set out for Pálos on May 12, leaving his son Diego as page to Prince John, heir to the throne of Castile. He found the trails crowded with refugees pathetically pushing handcarts piled with possessions. For European Jews it was a crisis not equalled until their persecution by the Nazis. Just at the moment when Spain needed all the economic resources and management skills it could muster, a royal edict commanded that all Jews be expelled. The result was that almost its entire professional class was on the run.

We can imagine a very different Christopher Columbus returning to reside with his friends at the monastery of La Rábida, which was only a couple of miles from Pálos. Outfitted with red finery, a gold chain or two around his neck in Genoese style, he must have been brisk, official and eager to be on his way. In the pocket of his new robe he carried three royal orders, and he wasted little time having the first read aloud in the Church of St. George at Pálos de la Frontera on May 23.

Pálos was a village of about six hundred on a grassy knoll overlooking an inlet off the Rio Tinto. Close to the Portuguese border, it was a typically rough little frontier community where seafarers scraped a living from smuggling, raiding Portuguese trading stations in Africa, fishing and running legitimate cargoes. With people escaping from one side of the border or the other and spies everywhere, Pálos people knew all that Portugal was doing and were hardened to high-seas passage-making.

The edict reminded the town's assembled leaders and officials of the fine they had incurred and commanded that two caravels, perfectly fitted out and manned, be made ready within ten days and put at the disposal of Columbus for a voyage "to certain parts of the Ocean Sea on errands required by our service." The crew were to be paid four months in advance. The royal order was met with respect but little else. On the day of the deadline Columbus had no captains, no pilots, no crews and no ships. He had run into what biographer Salvador de Madariaga described as "that tough Spanish nature which in the presence of royal orders had coined a masterpiece of undisciplined evasion: to be obeyed but not carried out."

Armed with the second royal order, addressed to all cities and villages on the coast and commanding assistance with the fitting out and manning of the vessels, Columbus carried his request to the neighboring ports of Moguer and Huelva but with equal lack of success. The reason was simple. He was already well known as a threadbare foreigner with crazy ideas. Years later, one sailor told how the local seamen and citizens "mocked him for pursuing such a plan and teased him and considered him mad." Besides, the local seamen were frankly skeptical that new lands could be found in the Atlantic and thought they could do better for themselves by joining in the sea-lift of fleeing Jews.

The enterprise was rescued from ignominy by the intervention of a local sea captain, Martín Alonso Pinzón, to whom Columbus was probably introduced by the friars. Esteemed for his seafaring and fighting skills, Pinzón had been as skeptical as the next man until Columbus produced convincing arguments in one guise or another. Whatever Pinzón heard, it fired his enthusiasm, and with his two brothers he quickly set about drumming up a crew. His influence made all the difference and, ever since, his role as Columbus's right-hand man and chief rival for glory has been a matter of heated debate, Spanish historians tending to exaggerate his importance and Italians to diminish it.

The town authorities finally complied with the royal order, but the two caravels they grudgingly supplied were the smallest they could decently get away with. This meant that Columbus had to look for a larger *nao*, or freighter, to carry enough supplies for the long voyage. In Puerto de Santa Maria he found a three-master of about seventy tons called *La Gallega*. The ship hailed from the Biscay coast and was probably waiting to load a cargo of wool for Flanders when her captain, Juan de la Cosa, agreed instead to charter her to Columbus. But it was not open-ended. The contract stipulated a voyage of 750 leagues (2,400 miles) from the Canaries on a course to be advised. When she sailed up the Tinto and dropped anchor off Pálos, Columbus decided to rename her *Santa María*.

At last things were coming together. Columbus himself would captain the *Santa María* with Juan de la Cosa as master, or second-in-command. Martín Alonso Pinzón took command of the *Pinta* with his brother, Francisco Martín Pinzón, as master. Another brother, Vicente Yáñez Pinzón, would captain the *Niña*, whose owner, Juan Niño, would be master. Columbus's staff included a secretary to write up the official proceedings, a royal official to keep track of expenses and look after the gold they found, a servant and an interpreter who, through his smattering of Arabic (thought to be the mother of all languages), was expected to engage the people they met in conversation. The marshal of the fleet, who acted as a kind of policeman

Without the support of Martín Alonso Pinzón (top) and his brother Vicente Yáñez Pinzón (above), Columbus might have languished much longer in the uncooperative port of Pálos.

and was in charge of the drinking water, was Diego de Harana, a cousin of Columbus's mistress Beatriz.

Nearly eighty men and boys ranging from veterans of the Guinea trade to green shipboys as young as twelve were persuaded to sign on as crew. Some served not only as seamen but as boatswain, painter, cooper, caulker, carpenter, tailor and goldsmith. In many ways they were similar to the crew of eighteen students from the nautical school in Cadiz who sailed in the replica *Niña* in 1990—home-town boys who had known each other much of their lives. The *Santa María's* crew of Basques—hard-nosed nautical men—had already voyaged together.

There was no risk now that Columbus would have to resort to his third royal order, granting free pardon to anyone accused or convicted of a crime, which would have enabled him to find a crew by scouring local jails. But he did sign on four men on the run who took advantage of the royal pardon to join the crew of the tubby flagship.

Through July the landing place at the head of the inlet below the church at Pálos was a scene of hectic activity as the *nao* and two caravels anchored out in the river were prepared and provisioned. The whole town played its part. Nearly a ton and a half of unleavened *vizcocho*, a bread made with salt to make it last, was baked in cakes as hard and flat as ceramic tiles. At least a ton of locally made, strong, golden-hued wine went aboard in large barrels for mixing in ever-increasing proportions with water as the latter became rapidly foul. There were big Arab jars of oil and vinegar for dressing salads, yard-long strings of garlic, bags of beans, chickpeas, lentils and rice.

Columbus also loaded fillets of fish that had been hung out on lines to dry in the withering sunshine and would be eaten in the Phoenician way with vinegar, and meat salted down in casks. Medieval sailors also carried little luxuries in the form of smoke-cured hams, ewe and goat cheeses from La Mancha, stone jars of honey or quince jelly and bags of raisins, almonds, apricots and figs. A few pigs and sheep were penned on deck for fresh food.

Finally came the boatswains' stores and trade goods. Spare ropes, pitch and canvas, large cooking pots and fire irons, lanterns and candles were essentials on any voyage. One headache for stowage were the long poles to be used as spars in case of accident. Into the *bodega*, or hold, went a big assortment of linen shirts, colored cloth and bonnets, little jingle bells (such as those fixed to the legs of hunting falcons), brass basins, strings of beads, mirrors, scissors, knives, needles and pins. This cargo of cheap trade goods of the kind used to buy slaves and gold along the Guinea coast is further evidence that Columbus was not expecting to run into sophisticated

Continued on page 107

(Inset) Columbus and his ships depart from Pálos on the morning of August 2, 1492. To the left is the Church of St. George where Columbus's men had heard mass before embarking. Below the church is the fountain where the ships' crews filled their water barrels. (Above) In Pálos today the old harbor has silted up but, aside from the addition of a tower, the Church of St. George looks much the same. The covered fountain still stands below.

Orientals, but primitive people similar to native Africans.

By the beginning of August the last bundle of firewood was packed away on the cluttered deck, the last barrel of water topped up. Probably at noon on August 2, Christopher Columbus, captain-general of the discovery fleet, celebrated mass with his crews in the Church of St. George overlooking the inlet. The salutations shouted across the water as the ninety men rowed out to their vessels were no doubt more high-spirited than sentimental, because seamen spend their lives making farewells, but one can fancy an undercurrent of dread. Ordinary seafarers and fishermen, nearly half of them teenagers and armed with no special quality but stoutheartedness, were embarking on a voyage toward dark realms where they believed no ship had ever sailed.

The three vessels moved down the river on the afternoon tide and anchored inside the bar of Saltés. Through the evening, boats pulled down the river with the last sailors and the last bits of baggage. Then, as the morning sky brightened, all hands tailed on the ropes to swing the heavy boats on board and lash them down. From the flagship's high poop, Columbus watched his crews slot the heaving-bars into the capstans. With an ebb tide bubbling under the forefoot, the men laboriously turned the capstans and hauled up the anchors. Then the captains shouted out, "In the name of God, make sail!" and in the pre-dawn light the pale sails rose up the masts with the sheaves squealing in the blocks like gulls. A special banner made for the expedition, bearing a green cross on a white background and the initials F and Y (for Ferdinand and Ysabel) under gold crowns, was run to the masthead.

The anchors came free of the mud and the ships drifted on the current. Long oars were manned, turning the ships to catch the feeble breeze. It was dawn on the morning of Friday, August 3, 1492.

By eight the little fleet was clear of the same sandbars Columbus had crossed seven years before on his arrival in Spain. Quickly the white beach of the low coastline dropped beyond the curve of the earth, and the distant blue hills vanished into the pearly haze. The little black-tarred ships were in their element at last as they danced to the lift of waves, and their sails and spars began to hum.

The disorienting contrast between the stresses of departure and the simple discipline of sea voyaging has hardly changed in five centuries. It takes time for men and ships to get the measure of each other and the routine of life under sail to establish itself. On the first day out there are inevitably a thousand little jobs but (as we found after raising our own anchor in the Bay of Cadiz on June 9, 1990) nobody knows where anything has been put.

By dusk on the first day, Columbus had already put behind him nearly 50 of the 750 miles to the Canary Islands. The first night at sea was a restless time as the crew settled into the simple routine of four-hour turns of duty rotated between three teams or "guards"—those on watch rotating their duties such as steering, calling the compass card and lookout. While the veterans sought a comfortable spot to sleep, claiming through seniority or sharp elbows the main hatch that was the only flat surface, others unrolled their sleeping mats in any space they could find.

For the young grommets at sea for the first time, the waves rising like monsters along the lee rail and subsiding with a hiss seemed doubly dark and scary. In every gust of wind they heard the grunts and curses of their shipmates slithering down the slope of the deck and the loud slap and gurgle of water racing along the planks. At a shouted command they ran to the ropes, bumping together in the wild, wet darkness, grabbing for handholds as the ship swooped sickeningly into a trough, their shirts rattling in the wind. The coils of rope swollen with water were heavy and stiff. Hauling until they thought their hearts would burst, coiling down, heaving, lurching, vomiting, nursing blistered hands, they were being baptized into the unchanging world of the seafarer.

We can imagine Christopher Columbus listening to the song of his ship with satisfaction, but whether he was patrolling tensely on deck or lying wakefully in the narrow bunk of the tiny cabin built for him in the corner of the flagship's poop, he kept his feelings to himself. However, at some moment during the first few days at sea, he sat down to a bureau fixed to the bulkhead, chocked an inkwell against the swing of the ship and penned at the head of a blank page, "In the name of Our Lord Jesus Christ."

The captain-general had begun to write a daily journal or log of his voyage, of the kind all pilots contracted to Portugal were obliged to keep for the benefit of the Crown. In that first entry Columbus described how he had witnessed the fall of Granada and summarized his commission to go to the Orient—not by the usual land route but by the Occident, or west, "which no one to this day knows for sure that anyone has gone." But after describing how he had found and fitted out the three ships, Columbus concluded on an enigmatic note:

. . . *In addition, Lord Princes, to noting down each night what the day had brought forth, and each day what was sailed by night, I intend to make a new chart of navigation upon which I shall place the whole sea and lands of the Ocean Sea in their proper positions under their bearings. . . which will be a great task.*

Is the word "new" a slip of the pen, and Columbus intends to make the "first" chart of the area as he goes along? Or does the word "new" imply that he already has a chart in his posession and is now intending to make a better one?

For three days there was little for Columbus to record as his fleet reeled off the miles, heading southward down the African coast. On the fourth day out he hit trouble. The *Pinta* suddenly turned into the wind and dodged over the waves, sails flapping and gear shaking. The caravel's rudder had lost two of its pintles, the iron pins that fixed it to the hull. The lowest of the three must have been still in place, or the rudder would have fallen off. The *Santa María* surged up to the crippled vessel, and the *Niña* altered course to see what was happening. But heavy seas were running, and they could only stand by while some of the *Pinta*'s men, hanging over the tossing stern, used bulks of timber lashed with ropes to build a frame

The ruins of the castle from which Doña Beatriz de Peraza y Bobadilla ruled the island of Gomera.

or collar around the head of the rudder to keep it vertical.

The *Pinta*'s captain, Martín Alonso Pinzón, told Columbus that the damage was the result of sabotage. It seems that the owner of the *Pinta*, not wanting his ship to make the trip, had sawed partly through the upper pins, which sheared under the press of weather. The scabrous cliffs of the African coast were only a few miles to leeward, but repairs were made and Columbus noted in his journal that Martín Alonso was "a man of real power, very ingenious." It was the only compliment Columbus would ever pay him.

The next day, the rudder gave more trouble when the collar ropes broke or worked loose under the strain. Worse, the *Pinta* also started making water. At daybreak on Thursday, when the volcanic peaks of the Canary Islands stood out on the horizon, Columbus made a puzzling decision. Ignoring the age-old custom that a mariner was honor bound to stick by another in trouble, he abandoned the crippled *Pinta* and her crew. He ordered Martín Alonso to make port as best he could, told the *Niña* to follow and set his own course for the island of Gomera.

With this one ill-considered decision, Columbus alienated his lieutenants and lost the trust of his men. As a foreigner with little experience in command, he had been laboring under difficulties enough, but now the captain-general had failed his first test.

Columbus's journal claims that he was heading for Gomera to find a replacement ship. This was a poor excuse to cover his actions. Nobody would buy or charter a new ship solely because the rudder was broken (it would be like buying a new car today because your old one had a flat tire). Besides, as the larger of the two caravels and the fastest sailer of the three, the *Pinta* was the handiest vessel in the fleet. Leaks in ships were routine (our own *Niña* made water for most of her trip) and could be easily repaired.

Maybe the real reason Columbus hurried ahead was the beautiful Doña Beatriz de Peraza y Bobadilla who ruled as "captain" of the island on behalf of her young son. A woman of not yet thirty who had been mistress to King Ferdinand, Doña Beatriz was known in Court circles as "the huntress." She had been maneuvered by Isabella into marrying the governor of this flyspeck on the map, where he had been killed by rebel natives.

Possibly Columbus (who knew Doña Beatriz from his days at Court) carried a letter for her from the king, but more likely he himself harbored a secret passion. At the start of his second voyage a boyhood friend who sailed with Columbus wrote that Doña Beatriz "with whom our admiral in other times had fallen in love" greeted his fleet "with fireworks and salvos of cannon." On that occasion, despite strict orders from the king not to waste a minute, Columbus dallied in Gomera for five days. Now, however, if he was hoping to show off his new status to the bewitching widow, he was doomed to disappointment.

Gomera's little harbor of San Sebastian was then the most westerly haven in the known world, but when the *Santa María* dropped anchor and a boat was sent ashore, Columbus learned that Doña Beatriz was away at Grand Canary Island. He was informed

Continued on page 113

A NURSERY OF CONQUEST

In 1492 Spanish soldiers in the Canaries were involved in a grim and cruel little war to tame or stamp out the Guanches and other aboriginal peoples who had occupied the islands for centuries.

When Columbus arrived at Gomera half the islands were yet to be subdued. The task of the military was exacerbated by the skill of the Guanches at fading into the land-scape. The islands were so lush that the Spanish farmers employing African slaves could harvest four sugar crops a year, but their plantations were constantly attacked by the dispossessed natives who lived in mountain caves.

Although Stone Age weapons were no match for swords and lances of Toledo steel, the Guanches held the Spanish at bay for many years with refined guerilla tactics employing rockfalls and fires.

This Spanish style of colonialism by conquest, in which native people were enslaved or slaughtered, proved to be a dress rehearsal for what would come on a very much wider scale to the other side of the ocean.

The Valéron Monastery, (above) also known as the Convent of the Virgins, is located high on a cliff on Grand Canary Island. The Guanche nobility kept their daughters in seclusion here until the age of thirty at which time these women chose either to become priestesses or to be married.
(Below) The mummified remains of a Guanche. Reportedly a tall, fair-skinned people, the Guanches had red or blond hair.

(Left) This bluff on the island of Hierro was the last land Columbus saw until his landfall in the New World.
(Top and above) The modern Niña *stopped at Gomera in 1990 and crew-members drew water from the same well from which Columbus replenished his ships' water barrels. Following the tradition of Columbus's time, a dinghy was filled with fresh water, rowed out to the ship and bailed into barrels on board. The water Columbus drew from this well is said to have "baptized America."*

that she was expected back hourly, but day followed day and she did not come. For two weeks Columbus waited but neither Doña Beatriz nor Martín Alonso showed up.

Finally Columbus lost patience and sailed for Grand Canary. During the night, as they passed by the island of Tenerife, a fountain of fire erupted from the 12,000-foot peak, spilling glowing lava down the mountainside. But Columbus calmed his apprehensive crew with accounts of the volcanoes such as Stromboli and Etna that he had seen in the Mediterranean. The two ships reached Grand Canary to find that Doña Beatriz had just left, while the luckless *Pinta*, having lost her broken rudder and been steered by laboriously playing her sails, had drifted in calms and struggled against headwinds for no less than sixteen days, arriving only the day before.

The port in Grand Canary was primitive, and no better ships were available, so Columbus decided the *Pinta* should be repaired on the spot by his own men. A new rudder was built, its pintles, gudgeons and other metal fittings forged by a blacksmith on shore. Meanwhile the vessel was beached and tilted on its side so the leaking seams could be caulked, then smeared with pitch.

At the same time the *Niña* was converted from lateen rig—tall and whippy triangular sails similar to those of an Arab dhow—to a square rig like those of the *Santa María* and *Pinta*. Historians have tended to assume that the *Niña*'s lateen sails had given trouble on the passage so far because following winds had caused her to yaw heavily, putting her in constant danger of a jibe (when the sail whips rapidly from one side to the other), which could have ripped out her masts. Wind directions were seldom mentioned by Columbus in his journal, but following winds on the first leg would have been unlikely. Yet the square rig was in fact ideal for the remainder of the voyage into mysterious waters far to the west, a fact Columbus supposedly could not have known.

After six days' work, both caravels were ready for sea, and they sailed back to Gomera where a handful of men had been left to collect firewood and stockpile provisions such as fresh fish and vegetables. The water casks were filled, and Columbus held a meeting with his captains and pilots. He ordered their ships to stay within sight of each other and to approach the flagship at dawn and dusk each day for new instructions. He was so sure that land would be found at a distance of 750 leagues that he pinned an important safety precaution on this assumption. After 700 leagues the ships were not to sail between midnight and daybreak so as not to run ashore in the dark. Also, he told them that the queen had offered a huge reward in the form of a pension of 10,000 maravedis a year as *renta de ojos* ("eye" money) to the first man to sight land; a special tax had been levied on the butchers of Seville for the purpose.

On the morning of Thursday, September 6, 1492, having knelt to pray in the Church of the Assumption which still stands in San Sebastian crouched under the island's cloud-capped peaks, Christopher Columbus gave the orders that turned the bows of his little fleet toward the unknown horizon.

BUILDING A CARAVEL

The new *Niña* was built in the traditional way shown in this fifteenth-century etching (right). Spanish shipwrights who had learned their craft in the days of sail laid down the ribs for the hull (far right). Shipwright's tools (opposite, left) have changed little over the centuries. Before the voyage parts of her hull were replanked (opposite, right) and caulked with oakum and tar. At sea with the trade wind filling her sails (below) the caravel was a masterpiece of the shipbuilder's art.

THE CARAVEL AT SEA

The caravel was a go-anywhere vessel developed by the Portuguese for nosing along the unknown coast of Africa. Built low and sleek, its shallow, narrow hull could hold little more than its crew and their provisions. But the lack of space was not important—the caravel's most precious cargo was the information it brought back.

Following Mediterranean tradition, the new Niña has "eyes" to help her see her way across the seas.

Large wooden deadeyes connect the shrouds, the heavy ropes that hold the masts up, to the deck.

For sailing against the wind it was usually rigged with triangular lateen sails like an Arab dhow, but Columbus's caravels from the Canaries westward had conventional square sails, to take full advantage of the steady trade winds.

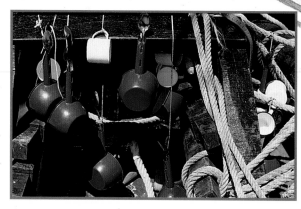

The modern Niña's crew hung their cups and pans from the capstan.

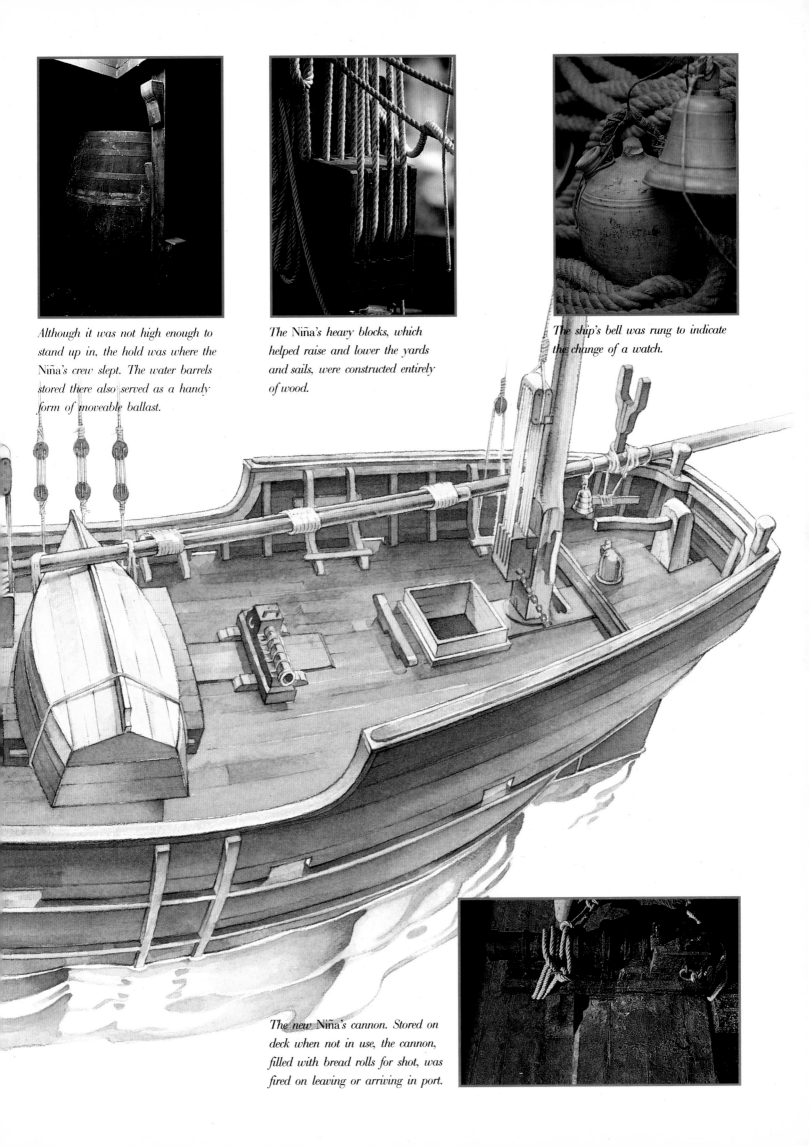

Although it was not high enough to stand up in, the hold was where the Niña's crew slept. The water barrels stored there also served as a handy form of moveable ballast.

The Niña's heavy blocks, which helped raise and lower the yards and sails, were constructed entirely of wood.

The ship's bell was rung to indicate the change of a watch.

The new Niña's cannon. Stored on deck when not in use, the cannon, filled with bread rolls for shot, was fired on leaving or arriving in port.

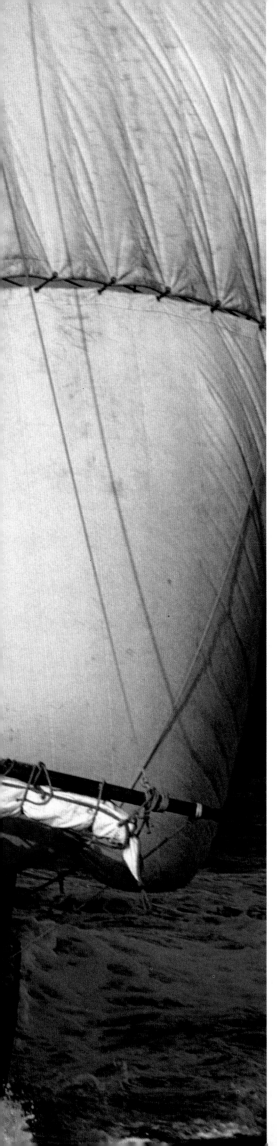

7 ONLY GOD CAN STOP US NOW!

*Across the Sea
of Darkness*

Spluttering a salute of smoky gunfire, the flagship and her consorts had hardly cleared the harbor and trimmed their sails when a Spanish caravel was sighted. It was rushing to intercept them with the urgent news that a squadron of Portuguese warships was lurking over the horizon to the southwest. Christopher Columbus had no doubts about their intentions. According to his journal, the king of Portugal was angry that Columbus had switched his allegiance to Castile and had ordered the warships to capture him.

The wind died, and for two days Columbus's fleet wallowed in calm seas. Shifts of sailors toiled at the oars of small boats, laboriously towing the ships in an effort to distance them from the enemy, while their disconcerted captain-general pondered what to do. Although he could not say so publicly, according to Dr. Coin, Columbus's intended route was not due west from the Canaries but southwest toward the Cape Verde Islands. Now that way was blocked. The waters south of the latitude of the Canaries were an exclusive Portuguese zone. If Columbus was caught trespassing there was little doubt that his ships would be taken as prizes, his men thrown overboard and he himself publicly hanged in Lisbon.

By the time the wind returned to fill his sails, Columbus had hit on an ingenious solution. His ruse would not only help him talk his way out of trouble if captured, it would succeed in confusing scholars and historians for nearly five hundred years. The stratagem Columbus adopted, as Dr. Coin's analysis of the voyage demonstrates, was to falsify both the directions and distances he sailed. In addition, as will be shown in the following chapter, his falsified journal was later deliberately scrambled to conceal key facts about the voyage and its discoveries.

The traditional notion that Columbus sailed west, always west toward the sunset until he was more than halfway across the Atlantic,

*With the trade winds filling her sails,
the new* Niña *heads for the New World.*

stems from the surviving extracts of Columbus's logbook, or *Diario*. Day after day it repeats the same phrase: "...they sailed on their course which was West." Until now, despite the puzzling anomalies of his description of this westward route, historians seem never to have questioned it. But the very fact that Columbus was so worried about the Portuguese caravels is the first clue that he was heading south. He had earlier tried to interest King John of Portugal in his plan and now the Portuguese were waiting just to the south of the Canaries to intercept him. This suggests that a westward route was never contemplated. Instead of remaining safely north of the boundary decreed by the Pope eleven years before, Columbus was planning to risk all—his ships, his enterprise, his life—by heading deep into the Portuguese zone. First, however, he had to sidestep the enemy ships, and that meant sailing west for a day or so.

The high islands of the Canaries at last dropped astern on Sunday, September 9. Despite the new breeze little distance was covered before nightfall. Columbus apparently reduced sail through the day to make the taller rig of the *Santa María* less visible to enemy lookouts. Once the flagship's crew had restowed some cargo to make her less heavy in the bow, the fleet licked along at seven or eight knots. The captain-general kept a close eye on the compass, and the log records that many times he rebuked the helmsmen—probably fearful of being sighted by the Portuguese—for letting the ship waver toward the north.

(Above) The ship's carpenter, using simple tools that would have been available in Columbus's time, made all the repairs to the new Niña.
(Right) The capstan, the ship's human-powered winch used for raising and lowering the anchors, provided a spot to rest between labors.

Of his change in course, probably to southwest by south, the log makes no mention. The only hint that something is not quite right, and that Columbus had deception on his mind, is the revelation that he decided to keep two accounts or reckonings of the distance traveled each day, the true one to be a secret and a false one of smaller figures concocted "so that if the voyage were long the people would not be frightened and dismayed."

This trick has become part of the folklore about the world's most famous discoverer, but how believable is his reason for it? It was never the custom for sailors to read a ship's official log, and ordinary seamen in medieval times were illiterate. Besides, Columbus had already told his captains that the first land would be found at 750 leagues, so the men already knew how far they had to sail. On the other hand, if the false account was to ensure that the official documents of his voyage maintained the fiction that he was in Castilian waters, the ploy makes sense.

During the Atlantic crossing he probably did keep two sets of distance figures. The fake distances he recorded each day in his official logbook and the true set he kept in his back pocket and planned to dispose of if capture by the Portuguese seemed imminent. Once his voyage was successfully completed he was able to insert the true

distances into the record alongside the false ones, adding the explanation that the latter had been part of his deliberate ruse to allay the fears of his men.

On the sixth day out, Tuesday, September 11, a lookout shouted that the mast of a ship was in sight, but it turned out to be only a piece of wreckage that Columbus thought had come from a ship nearly twice as big as his own. The weed growing on it showed it had been in the water a long time. As the fleet had by then covered 365 miles by Columbus's true reckoning, it would be hard to account for the wreckage floating in the clockwise current so far to the west of the Canaries. However, if they were sailing roughly in the direction of the Cape Verde Islands, which lie somewhat to the west of south from the Canaries, they would be close to Portuguese shipping routes. And there is other evidence that this was the actual route Columbus took.

Two days later, on Thursday, September 13, the diary noted that "the currents were contrary." This remark, which first set Dr. Coin on the quest to penetrate Columbus's smoke screen, is further evidence that the fleet was heading south or southwest. The currents due west of the Canaries invariably move more or less in the direction Columbus claimed he was sailing and could not have been against him. As the oceanic wind and current patterns are constant there is no reason to suppose that the situation would have changed in five centuries. Furthermore, from his professional experience Dr. Coin knew that oceanographers have identified a current that does set strongly to the northeast, flowing from the vicinity of the Cape Verde Islands toward the Canaries between the months of July and October. This could be the contrary current Columbus noted.

As well, Columbus reported that during the days since leaving the Canaries the water had been noticeably less salty than before. Historians cannot explain this comment. Samuel Eliot Morison concluded that it could only have been "imaginary." But it is hard to believe that veteran seamen emptying buckets of seawater over their heads to cool themselves down would be mistaken, and there is a plausible explanation to account for it.

Parallel with the African coast and roughly on a line between the Canaries and the Cape Verdes, there is a large area of upwelling where the cold and less salty layer of bottom water, originating in the Antarctic, rises to replenish the top layer as it is lost by intense evaporation and wind action. Had Columbus been west of the Canaries he would not have observed it. As well, the mixing of water due to the upwelling creates rich fishing grounds to this day. Columbus noted many tuna hunting in schools, and one was caught. As we sailed the same waters five centuries later in the new *Niña*, we, too, caught a tuna on a trailing lure, and those of us who cleaned our teeth in seawater noticed how remarkably less salty it was.

The birds seen by Columbus are another clue to his true route. On Friday, September 14, his log reported that the men of the *Niña* saw a tern and a tropic bird, "and these birds never depart from land more than twenty-five leagues." Columbus was wrong about the habits of these two species, but his comment is revealing. Although

Continued on page 124

The romance and the reality of deep-water sailing. Striking a pose out of the movies, a crewman handles the tiller. Above him another crewmember, hoisted to the top of the mainmast in a bosun's chair, carries out the daily check of the rigging.

his log puts him far to the west of the Canaries, he expresses no surprise at the birds' appearance. Yet the ornithological expert cited by Morison pointed out that the occurrence of the tern six hundred miles west of the Canaries is "incredible," while Bartolomé de las Casas, who knew Columbus well, noted wryly in his *History of the Indies* that the crew could not have been very experienced if they were seeing such birds in that part of the ocean. However, both the distance sailed and Columbus's comment would square with reality if the fleet were now approaching the Cape Verde Islands.

It drizzled a bit through the morning of Sunday, September 16, but the crews were happy and Columbus noted in his journal a phrase that would crop up every time he was content—"The weather was like April in Andalusia and the only thing wanting was the song of the nightingale." To judge by the latitude on which he later caught his first glimpse of a Caribbean island, Columbus had made his first turn to the west on the nineteenth or twentieth parallel. By now the dangers of capture were behind him, and the tension of the last few days was over.

That he was now sailing westward with the Cape Verdes astern is supported by another observation made that day. They began to see bunches of floating green weed "whereby all judged that they were near some island." The next day the weed became even thicker. Historians agree that Columbus was now entering the area of drifting weed known as the Sargasso Sea. But if he had sailed due west from the Canaries he ought to have encountered the weed much earlier, because mariners' reports dated early in the sixteenth century suggest that it lay considerably farther to the east and south than it does in modern times.

The gold and olive mats of sargassum weed floating in the current like sunlit rafts, providing shady umbrellas for hosts of fish, crabs and shrimp, cover a mid-Atlantic area roughly two-thirds the size of the United States. The spectacle of weed covering the ocean like a meadow made the sailors uneasy because they feared the ships would become jammed, but Columbus had seen it before on his high-seas voyages, and Martín Alonso Pinzón had been told of it by a Pálos mariner who had also worked for the Portuguese. Soon the men saw for themselves how easily the seaweed was parted by the prows of the ships and that it rustled lightly along the hulls without holding them back.

The fleet was entering the gyre of the North Equatorial Current which, on that parallel flowing from east to west like a broad moving pavement, hurried the ships forward and added up to forty free miles a day to their progress. Unlike a north-south current, which could be measured by taking latitude sights of the Pole star, an east-west current was much harder to detect because navigators had no

Traditional earthenware jars or botijos kept water cool, but drinking from them, as demonstrated by two members of the modern Niña's crew, takes practice. In Columbus's day the water grew increasingly bad and had to be laced with wine in order to remain drinkable.

way of measuring longitude. Columbus noticed the current but did not allow for it in his reckoning.

That Monday, the beautiful weather and good speed kept everyone cheerful. The fleet averaged 6 1/2 knots and according to Columbus covered 160 miles. The faster caravels dashed ahead of the flagship, hunting like terriers for signs of land to the westward. It was there, under the sunset, where Columbus expected that "God on High, in whose hands all victories are held, will soon give us land." With the Portuguese behind him, the wind filling his sails and his ships clipping along at a good speed, Columbus could just as easily have written, "Only God can stop us now!"

While the anomalies in the logbook itself support a strong circumstantial case for the route Dr. Coin has deduced, his theory is further bolstered by the accounts of contemporary chroniclers. For example, on his return to Spain, Columbus stayed in the house of Andrés Bernáldez who, in his *Memorial of the Reign of the Catholic Kings*, wrote that Columbus had left Pálos

> *. . . and set his course forward over the sea to the islands of Cape Verde, and from there always with the west [an obvious misprint for east] to the stern, he sailed toward where we see the sun set in the month of March, where all the sailors considered it impossible that land could be found. . . . and from the islands of Cape Verde they made sail according to the beliefs of Columbus. . . .*

The route is also described by Gonzalo Fernández de Oviedo, a royal chronicler who respected Columbus but supported the prime role played in the expedition by the brothers Pinzón. In *The Voyages of Columbus* he described the courses to follow to Hispaniola, stating that if a navigator

> *. . . does not come down to fourteen [degrees of latitude north he] will err to a great extent. . . and if he travels by nineteen or twenty, with chance of only a little unfavorable weather, and because of the defects of the compass needle, he*

*will not reach this island, and because of the currents will come
to land in the islands of the Lucayos or on the island of Cuba as
the Admiral [Columbus] did on his first voyage. . . .*

This is further evidence that Columbus did not head west directly from the Canaries but first sailed some six hundred miles to the
south, then turned west on latitude 19 degrees N or 20 degrees N
when he had covered about two-thirds of the distance to the Cape
Verdes.

On the evening of Monday, September 17, the compass needle
was checked against the Pole star and was found to have drifted a
full point to the west. This was alarming because the men knew they
would never find their way home with an unreliable compass, but
Columbus suggested the pilots repeat the test at dawn, and the needle
was found to be true. Columbus told them that it was only the star
moving, not the needle. In fact, what the pilots had observed was
magnetic variation—or the influence of the magnetic field on the
compass needle—a phenomenon then only sketchily understood.
Luckily for him, Columbus's explanation was plausible because the
star does move. The difference between the star's morning and evening positions was then about seven degrees (it is now less than half
that).

Five centuries later, as we ourselves voyaged in the same waters
watching the satellites gliding across the night sky until they were
hidden by the *Niña*'s billowing mainsail, it was hard to imagine ourselves in Columbus's world. Our compasses were much the same,
but while Columbus's was marked in thirty-two "quarters" of 11 1/4
degrees each, our compass card showed 360 individual degrees,
which made it ten times more accurate. He and his pilots could only
estimate the speed and distance traveled toward the west, and to
be within 20 percent of the truth was considered a good result. In
1990, sextant sights of sun and stars gave us pinpoint positions every
day. Magnetic variation was a puzzle to Columbus; we knew it exactly and allowed for it.

But, then as now, the ordinary sailor cared little. As we rolled
heavily through the bearded gray seas, it was surprising how swiftly the tiredness induced by tough and monotonous routine imposed
its own order. With a storm system tracking down the Sahara bringing gray skies and white-capped swells twenty feet high, every step
on the heaving deck was a fight, and we were on the edge of mis-
ery. Columbus's men were likely much less concerned with their
fears of the unknown or with falling off the edge of the earth, as
legend would have it, than with getting through the day. Like us,
they would have looked no further forward than the end of the
watch, the next meal, the next chance to sleep. Our student crew,
accustomed to square meals and modern comforts, probably found
it tougher adjusting to a life of wind and sun, but they soon lapsed
into the neutral state of mind of the sailor who does not think but
reacts—to the weather, to orders from the poop, to the half-hourly
ringing of bells that signals a change of duty.

In these conditions the mind feasts on details. The water-
softened skin that peels from the calluses on your fingers. The sparkle

*Working a caravel is a combination of
hard effort and waiting. Here, two
crewmembers wait to hoist a sail.*

of phosphorescence in the surging bow wave at night. The cry of *"Delfinas para la proa...!"* from the lookout as dolphins play under the bowsprit. No signs of life but the odd turtle passing along like a drifting green rock, or the purple sail of a jellyfish. One evening after dark a flying fish suddenly hit me in the chest; that night twenty-seven of them landed on deck.

For Columbus, as for us, it proved to be an easy trip—one of the most troublefree discovery voyages ever made. Not a sail was split, the weather was fair nearly all the way, nobody went hungry or thirsty and there was the odd dorado or tuna to spike the boring diet. Scurvy, which is caused by vitamin deficiency and would soon kill more men at sea than enemy action, did not appear because Columbus's voyage was relatively short. His crews were in good heart, nibbling chunks of hard bread soaked in water and wine, or improving their ration of stew with a dollop of vinegar. The veterans were accustomed to long voyages and later praised their captains, although they were still suspicious of the foreign captain-general. The trials of Columbus's first voyage to the New World would be neither physical nor practical but psychological. And eighteen days out, on Sunday, September 23, the first serious trouble began to brew.

By the end of this sailing day (counted from sunset to sunset) Columbus reckoned they had sailed 633 leagues, but the three pilots thought differently. It was their business to ensure the safety of ships and crews. Their necks depended on it. And it was prudent to overestimate the distances sailed; even modern navigators customarily assume that land or other danger is nearer than they think. Throughout the crossing the pilots in the fleet had estimated an average of 5 leagues per day more than their commander. By now their "plot" was substantially ahead of Columbus's and coming close to the 750 leagues where Columbus had predicted the voyage would end.

The crew of the *Santa María* had contracted to voyage 750 leagues from the Canaries, not one league more. As Hernándo Colón put it in his biography of his father, the sailors felt they had now tempted fortune as much as their duty required and had sailed farther from land than anyone before them. It was time, they thought, to turn around and commence the weary business of fighting against the wind to get home.

The journal entry for Monday, September 24, was uncharacteristically short, saying nothing but suggesting that something dangerous was happening. According to Hernándo's account, the grumbling went on all day. Through the thin partitions of his cabin on the small ship with its crowded deck, Columbus must have been aware of every word. Few miles were covered as the sailors huddled

Continued on page 131

The running rigging is made ready before the foresail is hoisted.

During a long sea passage in a wooden ship with canvas sails and hemp rope, minor repairs and endless maintenance keep the crew constantly busy.

(Left) At sunset the cooking fire illuminates the darkened Niña. The ship's cook prepares a meal of fish (above).

in angry little groups, plotting ways of turning around. We know from the testimony some of them gave to the *pleitos*, or hearings, held years later, that there were threats to heave Columbus over the side if he did not agree to their demands. It would be easy enough for them to report that the captain-general had fallen into the sea in darkness while observing the stars.

It was an explosive situation. The many Basques in the *Santa María*'s crew knew their rights. Even in the modern navy of Spain there is a saying that one Basque is a good man, but in a group they are dangerous. Columbus could threaten punishment, but what could he do, one man against forty? His promises of finding rich and beautiful lands just over the horizon were futile in the face of his crew's determined threat that if he did not turn the ship around he would not last the night. Columbus had no alternative but to order a lombard fired to signal the *Pinta* to approach the flagship. Then he sent his chart across the water to Martín Alonso Pinzón.

Whatever chart this was, apparently Martín Alonso had never seen it until now. We can imagine him scrutinizing it with fascination, probably copying parts of it for his own reference. By the next morning, Tuesday, September 25, according to evidence given at the *pleitos*, the pilots had calculated they had sailed at least eight hundred leagues. The master of the *Santa María* was her owner, Juan de la Cosa, who had as much interest as anyone in sticking to the letter of the contract and getting his ship home safely. No doubt he added his voice to the vociferous demands to head for home. But all hopes of turning back were dispelled when Martín Alonso Pinzón came alongside in the *Pinta* to return the chart.

Testifying at the legal hearings years later, one sailor said that Columbus and Pinzón agreed to sail on for another eight days, by which time they should have sighted the mainland that Columbus thought lay 1,150 leagues west of the Canaries. Pinzón then shouted across the water and warned the flagship's crew that this was an important voyage of discovery, not a trading trip. They must go on for as long as the ships had food and water and were free of disease. A fleet sent on a mission by sovereigns as great as theirs did not return without good news. "If any of you give trouble," he added, "I will come on board with my brothers and hang half a dozen of you from the mainmast."

According to the log, Martín Alonso called to the captain-general that he thought they were in the right position. Columbus said he thought so, too, but didn't know why the islands had not been seen. They probably discussed the extent to which the pilots had overestimated their speed. Columbus explained that even if they had missed the islands, by his reckoning the mainland was about eight days ahead, so they should continue for at least that long before reassessing the situation. Pinzón agreed. It was not long before they had the most convincing proof a navigator could ask for.

At sunset, when the haze of water vapor falls out of the air and for a few minutes visibility is at its greatest, Martín Alonso's eye swept the horizon from the poop of the *Pinta*.

Faint but unmistakable, an island was discernible on the horizon with the flare of the setting sun at its back. Not a cloud, not a mirage. "Land! Land!" he cried and claimed the reward Columbus had promised.

His men leapt into the rigging and peered ahead with eyes screwed up against the glow of the sunset. The news was heard in the flagship. Columbus checked for himself that the report was positive and fell on his knees to give thanks to God. Martín Alonso said the *Gloria in excelsis Deo* with his men. In the *Niña*, everyone was climbing the mast and rigging for a better look. "All declared it was land," Columbus reported in his log that night as he ordered sail to be reduced. The men leapt joyfully into the calm seas, and dolphins bounded toward them for a look.

The island sighted was almost certainly one of the small and insignificant islands in the Virgin group, outlying the northern end of the arc of the West Indies. Sombrero is the most likely candidate because it is the most northerly and is higher than its nearest neighbors, Anegada and Anguilla. All lie on or slightly below the nineteenth parallel, which fits the track Columbus would have been sailing. Spilling into the Atlantic by way of passages between the islands, fierce currents of up to five knots run toward the north or north-northwest.

During the night the three ships could have drifted forty miles or more without realizing it. The water is so deep in this region that it would have been hard for Columbus to detect the current by the usual means of dipping a long, weighted line over the side. For this reason, when anxious eyes scanned the sea at sunrise, the horizon was bare. The island had been swallowed up. The log dismissed the landfall as a mirage—"What they had been saying was land was not, but sky"—but is it likely that so many experienced sailors would be mistaken? In his *History of the Indies*, de las Casas told the story differently:

Until night everyone was saying it was land, and I certainly believe it was land because according to the track that was always followed, all the islands that the Admiral discovered later, on the second voyage, were in that strip or part toward the southwest. . . .

Since the friar's summary of the logbook is the only existing version, this assertion is even more arresting. But it is perfectly logical. He was alluding to the fact that this landfall (and, by implication, this route) was consistent with those of Columbus's three subsequent voyages when his track was known. On these trips he sighted land in twenty-one, twenty-four and sixteen days of sailing respectively. Now, on Tuesday, September 25, 1492, Columbus had been twenty days at sea since departing from Gomera. Our own landfall in the *Niña* replica was made after twenty-two days. But perhaps the most suggestive fact of all is a statement in his first letter home in 1493, quickly printed and disseminated widely throughout Europe and so never tampered with. In this document Columbus himself announced plainly, "In twenty days I found the Indies."

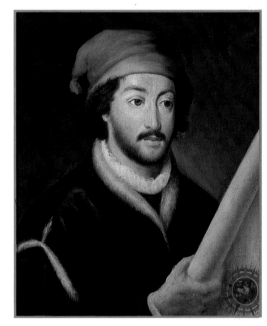

Juan de la Cosa, owner of the Santa María, *also acted as her master, under Columbus's command. (Right) A crewman keeps watch. Unlike Columbus's crew, the sailors of the modern* Niña *had to be on constant watch for other ships and floating containers lost by freighters.*

HOW COLUMBUS FOUND HIS WAY

In Columbus's time the main method of finding a ship's latitude was with a quadrant that measured the angle of the Pole star above the horizon.

Christopher Columbus was the world's first true ocean navigator. In the two decades before he set sail, all the major voyages of discovery on the Atlantic were southward. A navigator's chief concern, therefore, was to find latitude, which was done in a rough-and-ready way by measuring the height of the Pole star above the horizon

Safety regulations required the new Niña to use a modern compass which was much more accurate than the crude compass used by Columbus.

with a wooden instrument called a quadrant.

But for Columbus, sailing westward, accurate navigation required finding longitude. To do this, a navigator needs to know the exact time. But the most accurate clock available

to Columbus was a sand-glass turned every half-hour by a ship's boy. The best Columbus and his pilots could do was continuously estimate their ships' speeds, and keep a running total of the miles they had travelled. The effects of currents were ignored.

In fact, medieval navigation was an art rather than a science, akin to the modern-day sport of orienteering in which one follows a compass needle in a certain direction

and estimates the distance covered by counting steps. But Columbus's rudimentary compass was calibrated in thirty-two points, each of eleven and a quarter degrees, so it was inherently much less accurate than a modern compass marked in 360 degrees.

The compass was an uncertain instrument at best. It had no mechanism to keep it level in heavy seas, and little was understood about variations in the earth's

magnetic field, or of the influence that the iron in the ship itself had on the compass. Given all these limitations, it is not surprising that navigators in Columbus's time were happy if they were no more than twenty percent off in their calculations, and, indeed, a ten percent error was regarded as perfect pilotage.

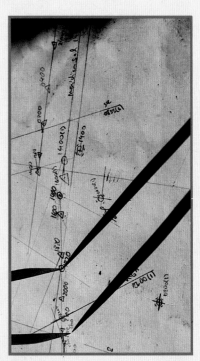

With dividers, the crew of the Niña plotted their exact position on the chart every hour.

At dawn and dusk, two members of the Niña's crew used modern sextants to find the ship's position.

(Opposite) The crew of the Niña kept an accurate record of their progress westward with the use of detailed charts, sextants, and digital wristwatches. Columbus's only clock was a fragile sand glass of the kind shown above the chart table at left.

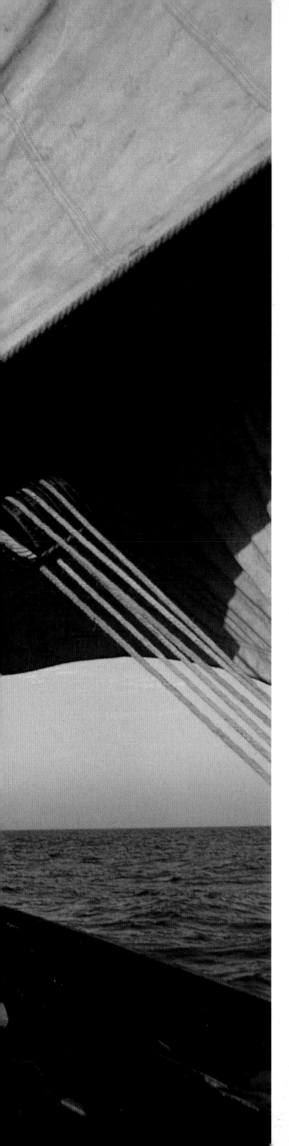

8 PRAY GOD AND HAMMER ON

Three days to find land or die

On his twenty-day crossing of the Ocean Sea, Columbus was unwittingly establishing the pattern of all east-west Atlantic voyaging under sail. Instead of heading due west from the Canary Islands as his logbook makes out, he sailed westward just long enough to dodge the squadron of Portuguese caravels waiting to capture him before turning roughly southwest toward the Cape Verde Islands. At about the twentieth or nineteenth parallel, as if he knew exactly where he was going, he turned west and sailed on until he saw land just where he expected it to be. That this was Columbus's true course is strongly suggested by Dr. Coin's interpretation of the incidents occurring along the way and by contemporary reports. But this is not the whole story of the falsification of Columbus's log.

As his ships ran down the trades, Columbus experienced some of the most enjoyable conditions known to blue-water sailors. The trade winds, strong and reliable unless disturbed by a hurricane, blow consistently and year-round from Africa toward the Caribbean. When Hernándo Colón, in his account of his father's voyage, wrote that for eleven days the ships ran under full sail "ever before the winds," he painted a true picture of the easy and delightful downwind sailing one would expect when Columbus's crew, like ours five centuries later, hardly had to touch a rope for days on end. Ever since, through more than four centuries when trade traveled on the wind's back, these permanent winds have carried vessels across the Atlantic; sailing yachts still enjoy their benefits today. Modern pilot charts compiled from many decades of reports from ships put the percentage of calms in these latitudes at zero. Yet the surviving summary of Columbus's *Diario* tells a strangely conflicting story.

According to the log, during his Atlantic passage Columbus suffered more than seven days of calms, flat seas and even headwinds.

On Wednesday, September 19, his ships were "becalmed," making barely three knots. The next day they changed course toward the north, because "the winds were variable with the calm that there was," and they made hardly one knot. Friday was "for the most part calm." Saturday and Sunday they tacked against headwinds. But these extraordinarily light winds, which would amaze any sailor with experience of trade wind voyaging, are only one of the log's puzzling features.

On Tuesday, September 18, when Columbus was about two-thirds of the way across, the log reported that he made more than 55 leagues (176 miles), implying a speed of more than seven knots. Yet the log also said, "all these days the sea was as smooth as the river in Seville." This is self-evidently contradictory. When we covered a similar distance at about the same juncture of our 1990 voyage, one of our best day's runs, the winds were fresh, heaping up large seas capped with white crests; anything less like a river would be hard to imagine.

Furthermore, on Friday, September 21, when describing seas again as calm as a river and the fleet creeping along at less than two knots, the log stated that the air was "the best in the world." This strikes a false note because a calm wind is hardly the best air in the world for a sailing ship burning up precious provisions and water while it rocks upon its own reflection. Until the invention of engines, sailors feared calms more than storms.

Throughout its days of crossing the empty zone of the mid-Atlantic hundreds of miles from land, both the log and Hernándo's biography reported the fleet sighting a succession of birds—pelicans, a turtledove, river birds without webbed feet, even a duck—that would be ornithological miracles if even half were true. On Thursday, September 20, for example, "they caught by hand a bird which was like a tern; it was a river and not a sea bird, the feet being like a gull's." Voyagers often encounter waifs and strays blown far from land (five days out from Gomera we were circled by a lone swallow), but on the same day, said Hernándo, Columbus saw no fewer than three pelicans and next morning "three little birds flew singing over the ship. . .which could not have come from afar." The men of the *Pinta* reported "a multitude of birds flying westward." In fact the Sargasso Sea, through which Columbus was sailing, is an avian desert. The lack of turbulence means mineral salts are not brought to the surface so plankton cannot be produced for birds and fish to eat. On our voyage we saw no birds in this area far from land.

Even more mysterious are evident signs of land observed along the way. While becalmed in drizzly weather on Wednesday, September 19, the log reported that Columbus "held for certain that in the northerly and southerly directions there were some islands,

The original of Columbus's log has long been lost. What we know of it today is a summary (with verbatim extracts from a copy of the log) made by Bartolomé de las Casas. This Franciscan monk also wrote of Columbus's first voyage in his History of the Indies, *a scathing indictment of Spanish policies in the New World.*

as in truth there were, and he was going through between them . . . ." On Sunday, September 23, they were astonished when the sea fell strangely flat despite the wind, but it changed abruptly to a heavy sea with little wind. This could be explained if they had sailed from the sheltering lee of an island that was out of sight just over the horizon.

None of these calms, headwinds, indications of land or absurd bird sightings make sense when they are reported to occur in the middle of the ocean. However, they would be consistent with reality if Columbus's fleet were nosing along the outer rim of the low-lying islands stretching northwest from his landfall in the Virgin Islands toward Florida—exactly what Dr. Coin concluded was the case for the second part of the voyage.

Similarly, many of the passages describing the second phase of the voyage seem to have been lifted from the mid-ocean section. For example, when we know Columbus was being confounded and held back by currents as he tried to penetrate the islands and cays of the Caicos and Bahama islands, we find log entries describing enormous distances covered. Through the night of Monday, October 8, they were said to be making up to twelve knots—though the sea was again "like the river of Seville"—and even de las Casas expressed doubts as he made the summary, adding in parentheses, "if the log is to be trusted." Such speeds, with daily runs of up to 59 leagues (188 miles) would, however, fit the early part of the voyage when Columbus was running down the trades.

Analyzing these and other nautical discrepancies, Dr. Coin concluded that many entries in the log have been scrambled. It appears that whole sentences and facts have been lifted from one day and transposed to another. The pattern turns out to be quite simple. Much of the entry made on September 18 has been exchanged with that for October 1, September 19 with October 2, and so on. Hernándo Colón's biography, which amplifies and adds to the inconsistencies of the log, follows the same pattern.

The manipulation of the journal was sometimes clumsy. On the day of the first landfall, for example, the log claimed the fleet made 4 1/2 leagues during the day and 17 leagues through the night, implying an average speed at night of 4 1/2 knots. This suggests that after sighting land at sunset, Columbus crammed on sail and raced toward unknown dangers in darkness. The suggestion is made even more preposterous when the log reports that after sunset the men went swimming, which would have been crazy if their ships were creaming along at such a speed. To sail fast at night when he believed land was near would have been insane and totally out of keeping with Columbus's stated policy.

If the figures were transposed without being changed, however,

Continued on page 142

A lookout aboard the new Niña strains for a sight of land as the ship nears the area of Columbus's first landfall. As on Columbus's voyage, a reward was offered to the first crewmember to sight land—in this case $1,000.

a more logical picture emerges. After making 17 leagues (55 miles) through the day, they sighted land at sunset and the wind fell calm as it often does in the evening near islands. Then sails were sensibly reduced and the men went for a swim, the ships making only 14 miles before dawn.

When the log is reassembled on these lines it gains an appealing new nautical logic. While crossing the empty zone in the trade wind belt, Columbus enjoys consistently favorable winds and makes good speeds but sees little wildlife (also our own experience in 1990). It is on the second part of his voyage after the first landfall that he encounters the birds, calms, headwinds and sea conditions typical of the Caribbean region.

Columbus is surrounded by a fearful and mutinous crew, demanding that he turn back. The men had contracted to sail for 750 leagues and were reluctant to sail any farther.

The rest of this chapter is based on the logbook as it has been reconstucted by Dr. Coin, on the likelihood that Columbus sighted an island in the Virgin group on September 25 but lost it again, and on archival documents. These include the testimony given by members of his crew at the *pleitos* or legal hearings held later, and accounts by chroniclers who heard the story from Columbus's own lips.

On the morning of September 26, with land no longer visible, the sails were hoisted but Columbus gave no orders to turn southwest toward the land that had been sighted the previous evening. Instead he carried on to the west. Only late in the day did he dip a few leagues south, but sighting nothing he resumed his westerly heading. Why he did not make a greater effort to relocate the land is unclear. Perhaps his "chart" indicated the dangerous reefs that are thick in the area. Whatever the reason, he behaved like a man who knew where he was going.

Was Columbus now intoxicated with success and justification? Land had been sighted just where he had always said it would be. Doubts about him evaporated, the threats were forgotten and the captain-general was regarded with a new respect. All eyes were turned ahead. What new excitement would be next to come over the horizon?

But apart from scanty clumps of weed, the occasional pelican and various other birds and schools of dolphins, the horizon remained empty, the seas smooth and the winds variable. The reduced amount of weed indicates that Columbus had passed out of the North Equatorial Current. The light and variable winds are typical of the fluky conditions of late summer in the Caribbean region. The sailors trailed lures for dorado—"fish with gilded backs"—and caught several that went into the pot. Soundings showed that the currents were tidal in nature, which could only have been discerned if they were near land.

For the next several days the three ships crept along on a

westerly heading, but their true progress was north of west, along the line of islands stretching toward Florida, but always just out of sight of them. They made good mileage by day, but each night they prudently reduced sail and were unwittingly carried to the west-northwest by currents. The Virgin Islands were soon left behind. Around the last day of September the fleet passed north of Puerto Rico without sighting it, then the Caicos Islands. The lookouts posted on the ships' mastheads saw nothing, and all found it strange that so many shore birds were seen but no land.

Dawn on October 1 brought a heavy downpour, then drizzle, the sea gray and sultry. Impatient with the slow speed of the flag-ship, Martín Alonso Pinzón dashed ahead in the faster *Pinta*, then heaved to and reported to Columbus that he had seen a big flight of birds passing overhead. Again the *Pinta* shot ahead and at sun-down saw on the horizon the thin black profile of a low and flat island—probably one of the Caicos group—almost covered by dark-ness and clouds. The captains and pilots urged the captain-general to turn away and look for the land but he refused. Columbus said he knew there were islands to the north and south, but "he did not wish to delay matters by beating to windward." Fearing to lose the initiative, he held determinedly to his original plan to sail west until he hit the mainland that existed, either in his imagination or on his chart, farther on. "The weather is favorable," he said. "We will press on and, if God pleases, everything will be revealed on the way back."

Discontent rumbled on among the crews through the drizzly morning of October 3, as more and more birds fluttered over the vessel toward the southwest, some of them singing, and the men even caught one in their hands. Still Columbus held his course stead-fastly to the west, believing that "[I] had left astern the islands which were depicted on [my] chart." This is the third direct mention in the logbook of the chart he had brought with him. Finally the grum-bling became serious and the discontent more dangerous because it was now rife not only in the *Santa María* but in all three ships.

The eight days were up. Columbus had promised Martín Alonso Pinzón that the mainland would be in sight by Wednesday, October 3, but there was still no sign of it. The men wanted to turn for home. Andrés Bernáldez mentioned this near-mutiny in his *Memorial of the Reign of the Catholic Kings:*

Seeing they had sailed more than one thousand leagues, and discovered no land, the sailors strongly held the opinion that there was no reason to sail farther because they were lost, and most thought it would be a miracle if they came back, and with sweet words Columbus and his captains persuaded them to sail on. . . .

Perhaps Columbus explained that he had counted on maintain-ing the same high speeds they had made in the Atlantic, but their average daily speeds had fallen by half due to the calms. Besides, he had been right about the first landfall, a mere island, and the main-land with a north-south coast would be impossible to miss.

The Pinzón brothers evidently accepted the captain-general's reasoning and when Martín Alonso made up his mind about

Flying fish landed on the deck of Columbus's ship, as illustrated by Theodor de Bry in the sixteenth century.

something the seamen followed. Eventually the crews were mollified and the fleet again gathered way. It was agreed that it would be silly to sail so far and not cover the whole distance to the mainland, but one can imagine the deckhands muttering to each other that the captain-general had better be right or he would find himself feeding the sharks.

The flotilla made the best of the sultry conditions the next day, Thursday, October 4. A whale was seen spouting nearby, and the boys amused themselves by aiming slingshots at birds using stones from the ships' ballast. Flying fish whirred out of the swells on "wings like bats," and on Friday, October 5, a squadron of them hit the sails of the flagship and thudded on the deck. It's a fair bet they were in the frying pan before they could blink. Piling on the frustration, a westerly wind sprang up, but Columbus turned it to his advantage: "This contrary wind was of much use to me, because my people were all worked up thinking that no winds blew in these waters for returning to Spain."

On Saturday the crew were still worried, saying that as the headwind was bringing no heavy sea, it would never blow hard enough to get them home. Then, to their undoubted astonishment, the situation reversed. The wind died and the waves increased. Such a situation can occur while passing close to islands in the aftermath of a brief storm: the ships were first sheltered in an island's lee, then exposed to the high seas when sailing out of it. These islands, invisible just over the horizon, were probably some of the Caicos group.

Now the distance estimates of the pilots, erring as before on the high side and surpassing Columbus's own estimate by 142 leagues, added up to a total of 1,193 leagues from Gomera. This was well beyond the mainland that had been promised, and again all confidence in the captain-general evaporated. The men became convinced that Columbus was a fraud who had misled them. Even Martín Alonso argued against his leader. Certain that Columbus's westerly course was a mistake, Pinzón wanted to follow the birds that flew to and from the southwest. But Columbus insisted, and Pinzón grudgingly went along for the moment. With the wind on its nose the fleet seems to have made little progress, and for every mile they struggled to the west, the current edged them about the same distance toward the northwest.

In head winds the caravels made better speed than the *Santa María*. A few minutes after dawn on Sunday, October 7, the *Niña* sailing far ahead was seen to round up and heave to. A flag broke out from her masthead, smoke puffed from her rail and a few instants later the faint boom of a lombard being fired carried down on the wind. This was the agreed signal for land in sight.

Continued on page 148

Slipping along in calm seas and light breezes, the new Niña experienced similar sea conditions to those encountered by Columbus as he sailed close to the islands of the Caribbean.

However, by the time the flagship had worked her way up to the caravel's position, the land was no longer in view. It would appear that the haze caused when the rising tropical sun sucked moisture into the air had reduced visibility to a mere four or five miles. But there is no reason to suppose Vicente Yáñez was mistaken. The fleet's third sight of land was possibly Mayaguana, a low and flat island surrounded by coral reefs in the Caicos group. And as the three ships clustered together for their morning conference, there seems to have been a terrific row. The Pinzóns argued it was essential to alter course to the southwest. The captain-general stubbornly ordered them to keep on to the west. While the crews anxiously awaited the outcome, the strong current carried the three ships even farther away from the land.

An hour before sunset Martín Alonso Pinzón decided he had had enough. The imperious captain-general, ignoring all the obvious signs of land and rigidly keeping his course to the west, was wrong. Pinzón ordered his men to swing the yards around, the course was changed, and making no further communication with Columbus, the *Pinta* sailed away in the fading light, following the birds that were flying overhead, one flock after another, to their roosting places beyond the southwest horizon. With little hesitation, Martín's brother Vicente Yáñez turned the *Niña* to follow. Having lost control of the leadership, Columbus had no option but to try winning it back, and he turned the *Santa María* in their wake.

Not surprisingly, the journal says nothing of this decisive incident, but testimony given in the *pleitos* was clear. According to one witness, "The Admiral stopped and Martín Alonso continued his navigation and the Admiral followed in pursuit. . . ." Another testified that "Martín Alonso made sail despite big danger and hunger and necessities and changed the course and because of this [he] found the Indies. . . ." And according to Gonzalo Fernández de Oviedo, who was later a close friend of Vicente Yáñez Pinzón, "Not one of them thought that on that parallel and course they would find any land." And once again, de las Casas contradicted his own summary of the logbook, saying it was only the impatience of the Castilian mariners that led the fleet to land where it ultimately did. If Columbus had continued he would have hit Florida, de las Casas added, noting that the westward route was very dangerous due to the reefs and shoals, while Pinzóns' route to the southwest was safer.

All night the powerful currents swept the three ships toward the open sea. All day they hammered doggedly on toward the elusive land. Unaware of the currents, they believed they were sailing very far to the west. On Monday, October 8, the men's nostrils prickled to the fragrance of land, while "twelve varicolored birds of the kind that sing in the fields" fluttered about the flagship. The next

The determination and pugnacity that helped Columbus face his hostile crew are captured in this sixteenth-century portrait.

day the wind was dead against them for a while, and the men sleeping on deck in the soft tropical night heard birds passing overhead. By now the crews were at the end of their patience. On Wednesday, October 10, the most critical day of the passage so far, the life of Christopher Columbus hung by a thread.

The fleet was now thirty-one days out from the Canaries, with only brief and indistinct glimpses of land. With strong winds blowing at their backs for most of this time, they had voyaged farther than any except Columbus himself had believed possible. The prospect of fighting their way back to Castile against those winds—their water supplies sour and dwindling, provisions getting low—was daunting. And as they neared Spanish waters again they would be running into winter. By the reckoning of the pilots, they had sailed 1,230 leagues and fulfilled more than either contract or duty demanded. To sail on now seemed tantamount to suicide.

According to the *Diario*, "the people could stand it no longer and complained of the long voyage; but [I] cheered them as best [I] could, holding out fond hope of the advantages they would have. [I] added that it was useless to complain; [I] had come to go to the mainland of the west, and so had to continue until [I] found it, with the help of Our Lord." As Oviedo heard it from his friend Vicente Yáñez, however, the story was very different. He spelled it out in detail in *The Voyages of Columbus*:

The men on board said in a shameless and public way that they had been betrayed and were lost, and that the King and Queen had used them badly and cruelly by trusting a foreigner who did not know what he was doing.

All three captains and the many sailors determined to head back [for Castile] and spoke between themselves of throwing Columbus into the sea, believing he had been playing with them. . . .

The feelings of Columbus at this desperate moment can be imagined. He had sacrificed so much and persisted for so many years to bring this venture to a successful conclusion and now, with the land he sought so tantalizing near yet still out of reach, he was faced with failure. Instead of a crew that cheered him on toward his goal they were hostile to a man. Martín Alonso, realizing the ships were dangerously close to the limit of safe return, joined the brewing revolt. Alone yet indomitable, Columbus bargained for his life, and never in all his long-winded sessions with kings, queens, princes, prelates, Court officials and scholars were his talents of persuasion put to a sterner test.

Reminding his captains and crews how much glory and profit they would earn if they carried on, Columbus pleaded with them to finish the job. He promised that in three days they would find what they were looking for. And he staked his life on it. In the event that there was no land, he said, they could do what they wanted.

It must have been a masterly performance. Even Columbus admitted later in a letter that he was inspired by God; de las Casas thought "God had held his hand." His words moved the hearts and resolve of everyone, especially the three Pinzóns. They agreed to sail those three days "with determination and harmony," but not one hour more. They thought nothing Columbus said was certain, according to Oviedo, and "refused unanimously to go farther, saying they did not want to die." The main reason for their fear was the shortage of food and water which, even if rationed, would not last them all the way back to Spain.

That Columbus was in no doubt of the penalty of failure is evident from the account given by Peter Martyr, the Milanese counselor to the Catholic Kings, who heard the story from Columbus himself, his personal friend:

A nineteenth-century artist's depiction of the moment when Columbus hears that land has been sighted.

His Spanish companions first began to grumble in low voices, then speaking insults to his face; finally [Columbus] thought he was going to be killed or thrown into the sea: they said they had been deceived by [Columbus], and they were heading for an abyss from which they would never return. After these thirty days, blind with anger, they beseeched him to go no further but to go back. . . . With gentle persuasion and big promises he saw their anger giving way; he pointed out that the Sovereigns would punish them for treason if they tried to do something against him or did not obey him. . . .

Having spent a good part of the day in argument while the current relentlessly carried them away from the land they sought, the fleet gathered way once more. Through Thursday, October 11, the signs of land increased. As the ships plugged on, making between four to six knots in the variable winds that can be expected near the islands, a green reed was seen floating in the water. The *Pinta* picked up a little stick that seemed to have been carved with a sharp blade, as well as a plant and a piece of board. The *Niña* collected a twig with little flowers which Columbus took for wild dog roses; his son later described it as a thorn branch loaded with red berries which seemed to be freshly cut. "With these signs everyone breathed more freely and grew cheerful," the log related, and in the circumstances Columbus himself was no doubt more cheerful than most.

In a strong breeze the fleet sailed swiftly but cautiously onward, every pair of eyes peering ahead. Even when the sun went down they pressed on. That Columbus continued sailing swiftly through the darkness is perhaps a sign of his desperation. Then, at two o'clock in the morning on Friday, October 12, the crack of a lombard was heard from the *Pinta,* which was scouting ahead as usual.

By the light of the three-quarter moon a sharp-eyed seaman called Juan Rodriguez, from Triana in Seville, had sighted breakers bursting along a low, rocky shore. All saw the long, low, dark bulk of land about 2 leagues (6 1/2 miles) to the north. At once sails were let loose and the headlong dash of the three ships abruptly halted. The *Santa María* caught up with the *Pinta,* and the *Niña* closed in. Under reduced sail the little squadron heaved to, marking time until dawn revealed a safe way forward.

During those few hours, as the three ships of Christopher Columbus rode easily over the waves but made no headway, and the captain-general and his men cast many a curious glance at the dark blur of unknown land, human history was on the verge of a momentous event. On the island under the moonlight the natives in their huts were unwittingly enjoying the last sleep of their innocence. As much as the men on the three ships, they would wake the next morning to a new world. Two great branches of the human race would at last be brought face to face. But the discovery began as it would continue—in dishonor.

Letting his Genoese petulance surface, Christopher Columbus decided to deprive Juan Rodriguez of the pension of 10,000 maravedis a year *renta de ojos* that the sovereigns had promised. In his journal Columbus claimed that he himself had seen land four hours earlier. While standing on the poop he saw a light, "so uncertain a thing that he did not wish to declare it was land...like a little wax candle lifting and falling." His servant, who must have known on which side his bread was buttered, confirmed the sighting, but the royal comptroller did not. Nor did any of the sailors who were looking out so keenly.

The only possible conclusion is that the captain-general's claim was a contemptible fabrication. Had he really seen a light, he would never have continued to sail pell-mell toward an unknown shore in darkness. This would have been contrary both to his own orders and to all nautical sense, as shown by the fact he did stop as soon as land was sighted. Instead he continued onward for four hours, during which the log implies the fleet covered well over thirty miles. To this must be added the six miles that stood between the ships and land when Rodriguez made his sighting. No light at sea ever could be seen at that distance. Some writers have suggested that the light was an Indian moving with a torch from one house to the next. De las Casas wryly speculated that it was a native with a firebrand lighting his way to and from a place "to comply with the natural necessities." But even the lamp of a tall modern lighthouse is not seen over the horizon nearer than about twenty miles. A bonfire on shore would have been hidden by the curve of the earth and native boats did not fish in deep ocean so far out. But for now Columbus said nothing. The decision to claim the glory and the reward for himself was still only brewing in his mind.

As the moon set and the sky slowly brightened in the east, the three ships of Christopher Columbus waited to see what daylight would bring.

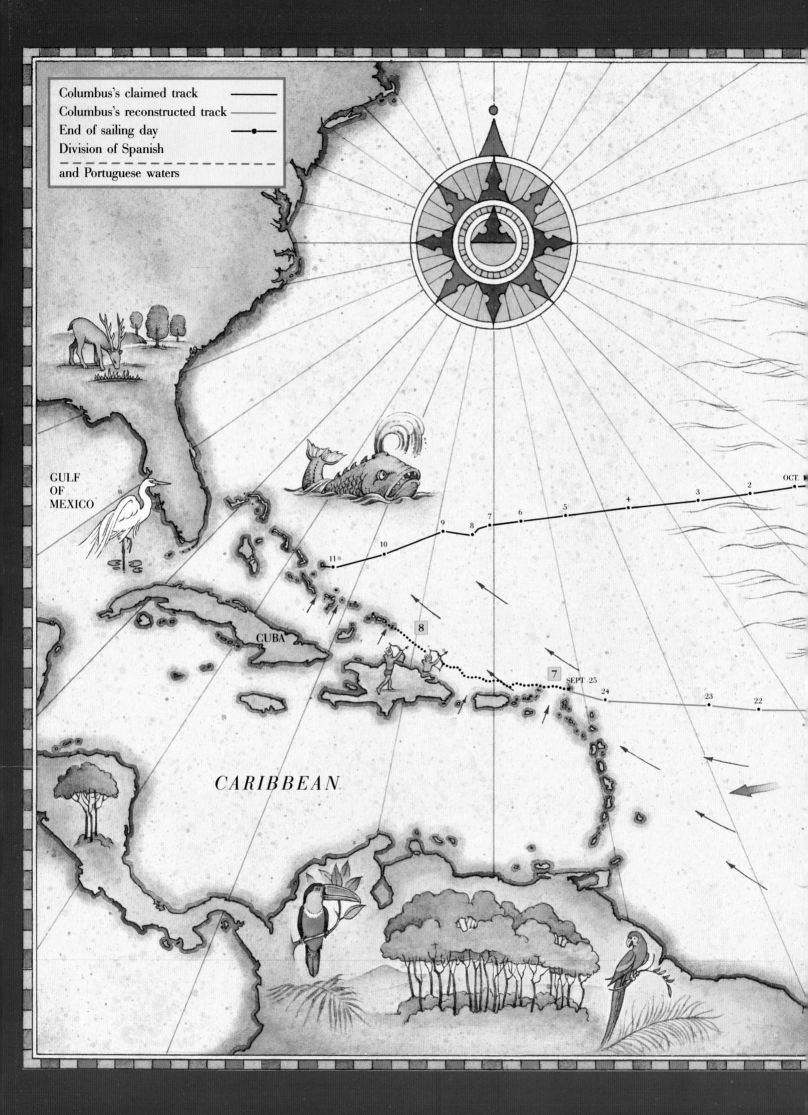

Columbus's claimed track

Columbus's reconstructed track

End of sailing day

Division of Spanish
and Portuguese waters

GULF
OF
MEXICO

CUBA

CARIBBEAN

OCT.

SEPT 25

THE NAUTICAL EVIDENCE: HOW COLUMBUS CROSSED THE ATLANTIC

1 *Columbus complained of contrary currents that do not exist west of the Canaries where he said he was sailing, but the current would have been against him had he been heading south. Such nautical clues collected by Dr. Luís Coín, himself a master mariner, suggest Columbus falsified his ship's log to conceal his true route deep into Portuguese waters where capture would have meant death.*

PORTUGAL

SPAIN

1000

COLUMBUS'S ROUTE TO THE NEW WORLD

The traditional notion, based on his shipboard log, is that Columbus steered west from the Canary Islands and, dipping slightly south, sailed on until he found land.

But the nautical information in the log, as well as contemporary accounts, suggest the true route of Columbus lay further south, closer to the routes he took on his second, third and fourth voyages.

It seems that Columbus kept a false account in his log so that, if captured by the Portuguese, he could claim he had no intention of trespassing in the exclusive zone granted them by the Pope.

That Columbus would risk so much to sail into enemy waters bolsters the theory that he was not inspired by a wild idea, but following a secret map.

The nautical clues that alerted Dr. Luís Coin Cuenca to the puzzling inconsistencies of Columbus's log are illustrated in this map of his false and true routes.

1 Four days out from Gomera, a lookout spots part of a ship's mast drifting on the surface. Given the generally clockwise pattern of Atlantic currents, it is unlikely such wreckage would be found west of the Canaries rather than to the south, in waters frequented by the Portuguese.

2 Columbus complains the current is contrary. It seems he was being slowed by the current which flows northeastward from the Cape Verde Islands between June and October. Had Columbus been sailing west, the current would have been favorable.

3 Columbus claimed that the sea water was "less salty by half." Historians have dismissed this observation as imaginary, but if he were sailing south toward the Cape Verdes, Columbus would have crossed an area of "upwelling" where a deep layer of fresher water, originating in the Antarctic, comes to the surface.

4 Columbus sees numerous dolphins and tuna. The mixing of water caused by upwelling creates rich fishing grounds that do not exist west of the Canaries.

5 On September 14, a tern and a tropicbird are sighted and Columbus observes that these birds do not fly more than twenty-five leagues from land. Although Columbus was mistaken about their ranges, his comment suggests he knew that land was within about eighty miles. According to Dr. Coin, that land was the Cape Verde Islands, the northern limit of the tropicbird's breeding zone.

6 After turning westward and leaving the Cape Verdes astern, Columbus's ships run into Sargasso weed. Archival documents suggest that this weed once spread farther east than it does today, and Dr. Coin believes if Columbus had headed west from the Canaries, he would have run into it days earlier.

7 "In twenty days I found the Indies," Columbus writes in his first letter home. This landfall is consistent with the southern track and his subsequent voyages. If Columbus were sailing westward from the Canaries, it cannot be true. Coin believes the log was later amended to describe his landfall as a mirage so as to discredit Martín Alonzo Pinzón. But Columbus himself reported of his experienced mariners, "All said it was land."

8 Historians have long glossed over the many puzzling features of Columbus's log. If Columbus were sailing west from the Canaries, as he claimed, how could he have seen land where none exists, and hit headwinds and calms in the trade wind belt? Dr. Coin believes that long after the voyage the log entries written in the middle of the Atlantic were switched with those written later, when the fleet was struggling in fluky conditions near the islands. The shadowy sightings of land, headwinds, calms, large flocks of birds flying overhead and visits from pelicans, a duck and "singing birds from the land" are all consistent with what ships would have experienced as they crept along the outer rim of the Caribbean toward the landfall island of Guanahaní.

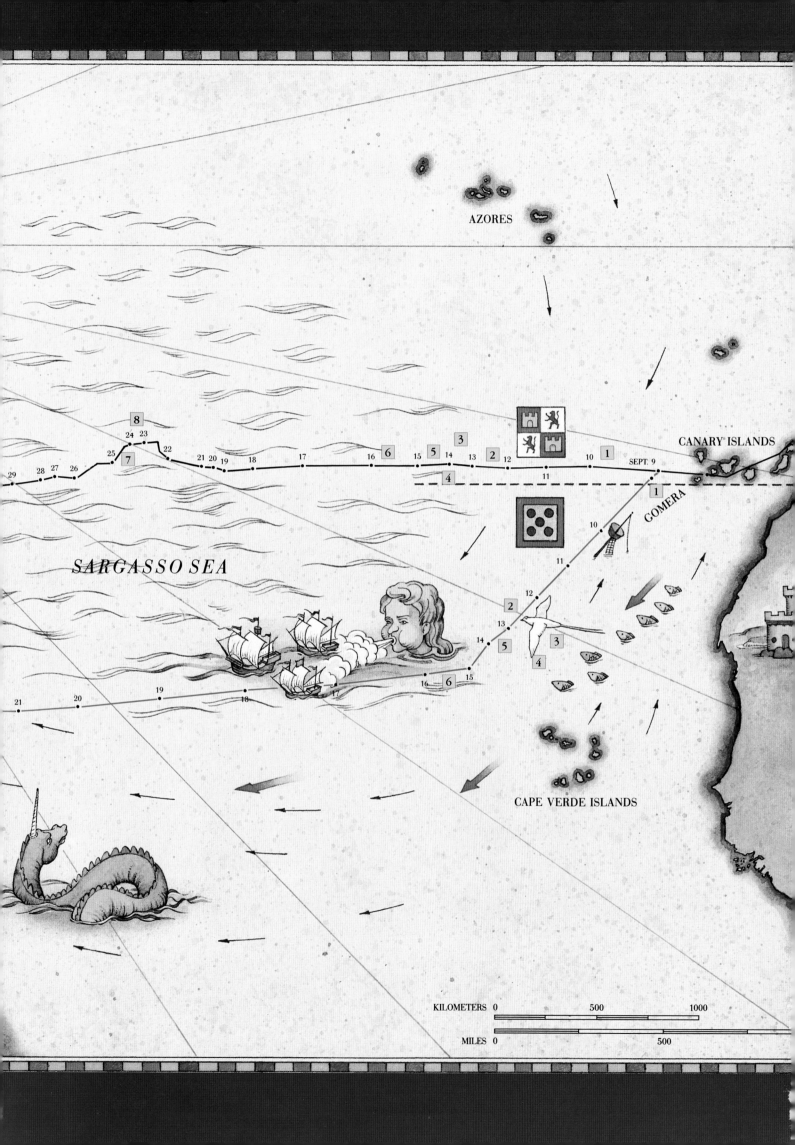

AZORES

CANARY ISLANDS

SARGASSO SEA

GOMERA

SEPT. 9

CAPE VERDE ISLANDS

KILOMETERS 0   500   1000

MILES 0   500

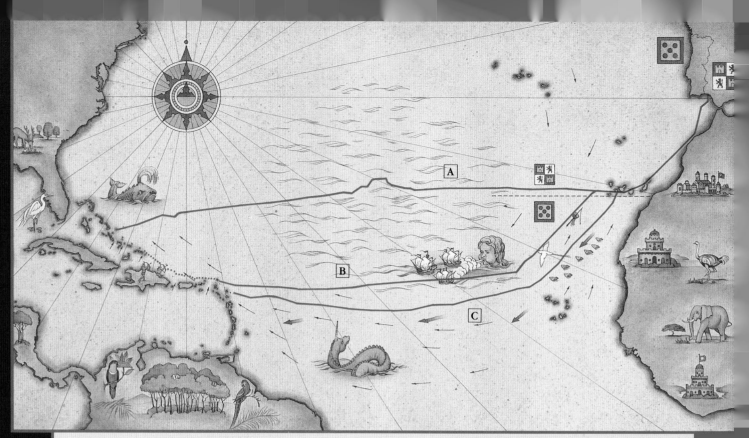

Columbus's claimed track (A). The reconstructed track (B) is close to that of his subsequent voyages. The track of the Niña in 1990 (C), forced southward by heavy swells.

3 Columbus hooked one of the many tuna he saw, a sign that he was not west of the Canaries but in the rich fishing grounds created by oceanic upwelling toward the south.

4 Drifting mats of Sargasso weed, more extensive in Columbus's day, point to his more southerly track.

2 In the early days of the trip the Niña's crew, like Columbus's men, noticed a fresher taste to the seawater—a sign of the upwelling of less salty water that occurs off the African coast.

5 A booby circles the Niña as she nears land. Columbus's mid-ocean sightings of pelicans and even a duck are clearly impossible. But if he were sailing along the chain of islands, big flocks of land-based birds would have been common.

6 Evidence that Columbus's diary is not what it seems is his reference to men splashing over the side while their ships were moving at above five knots. The new Niña's crew dared to swim only when the caravel was dead in the water.

7 Sighting land but losing it again on the twentieth day, Columbus hit calms and headwinds as he sailed along the barrier of the Caicos and Bahama Islands. With currents pushing him seaward, land remained tantalizingly out of reach.

The blast of a cannon signals that land is in sight. Columbus's ships fired lombards, an early kind of cannon, to inform the others when land had been spotted.

9 VISITORS FROM THE SKY

Search for Gold in a World of Wonders

Sunrise revealed an unimportant scrap of land of breathtaking beauty: a rather flat, tropical island ringed with white beaches, covered with lush green forest and set in a blue sea. The joy and curiosity with which the seafarers gazed at it from perches in the rigging can be imagined. Through most of the day the ships made a cautious approach, coasting around the far tip of the island, then gliding into the smooth water in its lee. All feasted their eyes on emerald trees thick with screeching birds. They peered into turquoise depths where brilliant fish finned among mushroomheads of coral and sang out in astonishment when a handful of naked men, their brown skins painted black, white and red, appeared on the dazzling beach.

Where a break in the reef gave access to the shore, three anchors plunged into the bottle-clear water. Yards were lowered and sails furled, the natives watching as the great "birds from the sky" folded their white wings. Boats were heaved over the side, and Christopher Columbus disembarked in all his finery. As the boat ran onto the beach he stepped ashore at the head of a procession of men carrying arms and banners and, falling to his knees on the sand, gave thanks to God. Then, erecting a Holy Cross and gallows as symbols of faith and justice, and cutting a handful of grass to represent his taking control of the land, Columbus formally claimed it in the name of the Queen of Castile and named it San Salvador (Holy Savior).

Columbus had landed on one of the forty islands and six hundred cays in the Bahama and Caicos groups which stretch like a partly submerged barrier reef across the approaches to the Caribbean. The natives called it Guanahaní, but its precise identity remains a question of heated debate.

"The whole [of the island] is so green that it is a pleasure to gaze upon," Columbus wrote, "and this people are very docile." Soon the trusting islanders were swimming to the ships or paddling out in one of the many dugouts (which Columbus noted they called a *canoa*), bringing hanks of cotton, spears tipped with fish bones and tame parrots to trade for bits of broken crockery and glass. He was thrilled by the gold ornaments the awestruck Taino "Indians" wore in their noses, and the readiness with which they exchanged them for the glass beads, red caps and tiny hawks' bells he handed out. One of the natives, having never seen a weapon forged from iron, took a Spanish sword by its blade and was amazed by the blood streaming from a cut in his hand. Columbus described their fine faces, handsome bodies, good stature, lack of paunch and quick intelligence. "They ought to be good servants and of good skill," he added, and kidnapped six whom he shackled to his deck.

But the log makes no mention of the blazing argument that erupted, according to sailors testifying in the *pleitos*, when Columbus made it known he was depriving the sailor Juan Rodriguez of his rightful reward and keeping it for himself. Compounding his evident lack of skill in managing men, Columbus also banned his sailors from trading with natives on their own account, saying all gold and spices were a royal monopoly under his control. Thus he canceled all the promises of "great wealth" with which he and Martín Alonso had encouraged the men to sign on.

It is hardly surprising that Columbus would be reluctant to leave his flagship after this. His friend Peter Martyr said he did not step off the *Santa María* until she sank beneath him, and Gonzalo Fernández de Oviedo heard from one of the sailors that Columbus did not set foot ashore again until the fleet was careened in Cuba. With his titles of admiral, viceroy and governor now assured, it is likely the expedition leader delegated scouting and exploratory trips to his pilots and sailors rather than put himself in danger of snakes, alligators, reefs, unruly natives and other perils. In light of the hostility and resentment he had generated, it would also have been prudent not to separate himself from the flagship and royal officials, his power base.

Columbus was in a fever to locate the source of the natives' gold, and when he questioned them by sign language they indicated with airy waves of the hand a southwesterly direction. As well, it seems that the lake or lagoons on the island were brackish, and it was urgent to replenish the ships' foul-tasting and dwindling supplies. On the third day, after a handful of men commanded by one of the masters or pilots had sailed halfway around the island in a boat and found a wide, calm harbor with an ideal site where a fort could be built to guard it, Columbus weighed anchor and set course to the southwest. Almost at once the horizon was dotted with so many islands that he could not decide which one to visit first. He headed for the largest.

So began the first Caribbean holiday. For three months the flotilla rambled amid a world of marvels and enchantment, never stopping long, always moving on to where the promise of gold was brighter. Like some millionaire modern tourist, Columbus dispensed

Continued on page 168

The first New World people to meet Columbus were Tainos. Columbus commented on their good stature and physical condition, adding ominously, "they ought to be good servants and of good skill."

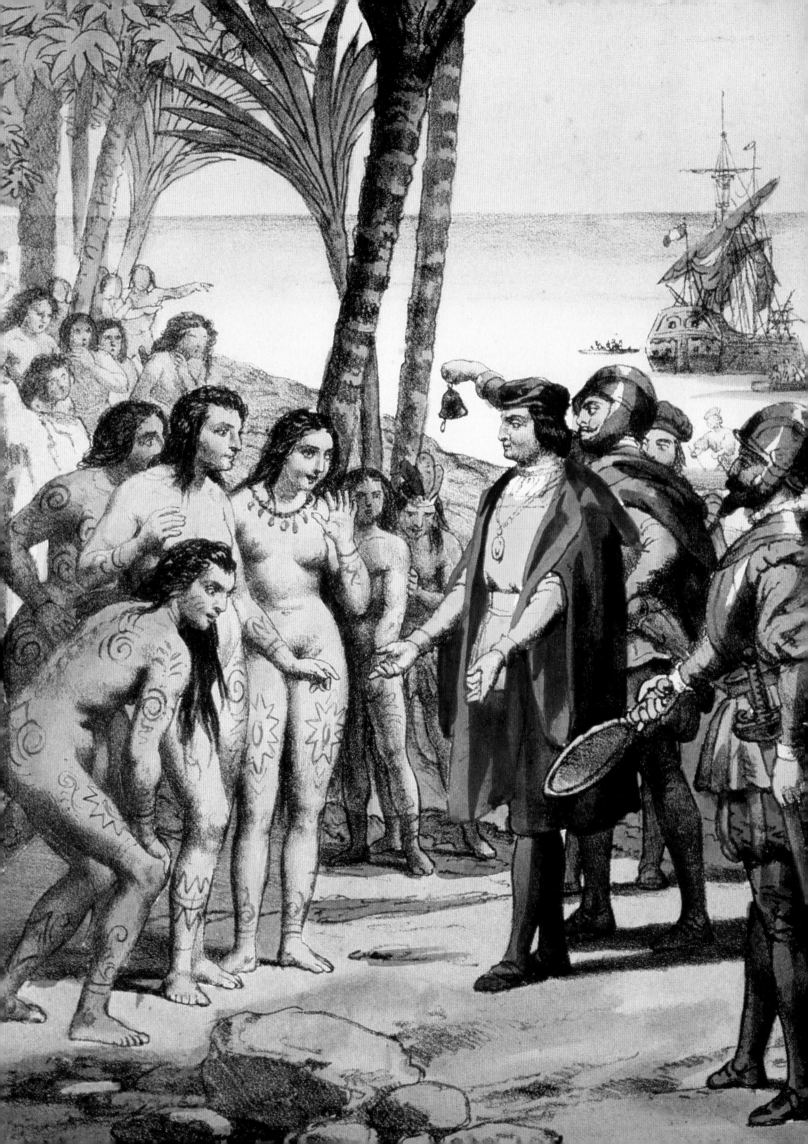

WHERE DID COLUMBUS LAND?

The island known by its people as Guanahaní and named San Salvador by Christopher Columbus on October 12, 1492, was said to be quite large and very flat, with a lake or lagoon in the center. But the footprints in the sand of Guanahaní quickly vanished and the identity of the most celebrated landfall in history remains a 500-year mystery.

No map of the island survived and Columbus's own account, rife with ambiguities and omissions, does not pinpoint the location precisely. His description could fit many of the several hundred low-lying palmy islands and cays which stretch like outriders of the Caribbean in a 375-mile chain roughly between Florida and Puerto Rico.

Over the last two centuries scholars have proposed no fewer than nine islands and cays as the landfall of Columbus, but most of these have been discounted. Today, a heated historical controversy focuses on three—Watling Island (officially renamed San Salvador in 1926), Samana Cay and Grand Turk.

To pin a precise identification to the map, investigators draw mainly on three sources of evidence.

1 The first of these involves following the Atlantic track, the obvious method, but in many ways the least reliable. Until now, all theorists have assumed that Columbus sailed directly westward from the Canary Islands until he sighted land after thirty-three days. But

Dr. Coin's theory now casts serious doubt on that assumption. Even if he did take this route, a ship's speed, and thus the distance it covered, was estimated by eye and precision depended entirely on the pilot's judgement. In pilotage of the Columbus period, accuracy to within twenty percent was acceptable and ten percent was "perfect." With these limitations the Atlantic track, therefore, cannot be recreated with an accuracy sufficient to differentiate between islands less than one hundred miles apart.

2 The second set of clues concerns the landfall island itself which Columbus described vividly but in vague geographic terms. For

example, he said the island was "very level" and "with no mountain": San Salvador is not as flat as Samana Cay or Grand Turk, but it is far from level with dune-like hills rising to 140 feet. After his long voyage it was urgent that Columbus replenish his water supplies but he did not do so until he reached another island several days later. This is an argument in favor of Grand Turk because its lakes are brackish while Samana Cay and San Salvador have abundant fresh water in October.

3 A third way to identify the landfall island is to backtrack along his later route. In the two weeks after Guanahaní, Columbus called at three more main islands which he baptized Santa Maria de la Concepcion, Fernandina and Isabella. The "fit" of the complex series of courses and distances sailed is disputed because Columbus's log is vague on crucial navigational detail.

Every landfall theory depends on interpretations that are wide open to argument. To make their theories fit, some scholars claim that Columbus himself, or medieval copyists, made gross errors such as writing "miles" when they meant "leagues" or *leste* (east) instead of *oueste* (west). To establish Watling Island as the landfall, the eminent historian Samuel Eliot Morison claims that when measuring distances along the shore, Columbus shortened the league he used from just over three miles to about one.

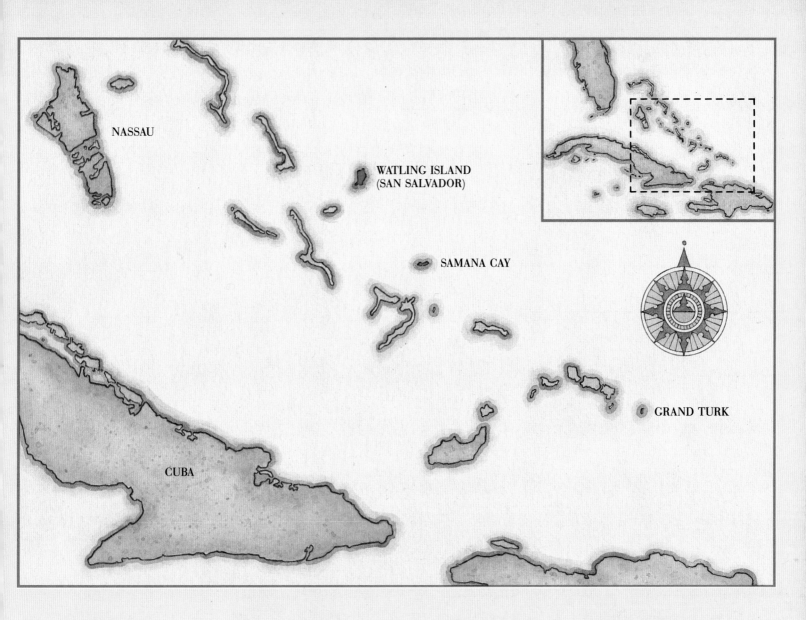

WATLING ISLAND (SAN SALVADOR)

Generally accepted for more than a century, this outpost of the Bahamas is quoted in most textbooks, encyclopedias and maps as the landfall island. In May 1987, without considering contrary evidence, a meeting of Ibero-American countries "officially" confirmed San Salvador as the landfall. In light of new research and interpretations of the log, however, the San Salvador theory looks increasingly shaky.

SAMANA CAY

In its November, 1986 issue, the *National Geographic* *Magazine* identified this uninhabited island sixty-three miles southeast of San Salvador as the "true" landfall. It was the endpoint of a voyage sailed across the Atlantic and another, simulated by computer, that back-tracked through the islands. Described as "probably the most important in our history," this article did much to demolish the Morison theory but the Samana alternative was attacked from many sides and soon looked equally tenuous. The magazine's aerial photograph of Samana showed big swells rolling over a submerged reef into a narrow lagoon that would hardly have struck a sailor like Columbus as a deep and roomy port "where the sea does not move more than within a wall." The harbor with two mouths, as Columbus described another anchorage, clearly has three as the magazine's own picture confirms.

GRAND TURK ISLAND

This landfall in the Turks and Caicos group, 170 sea-miles southeast of Samana, was first proposed in 1825. Because Grand Turk is too far south and there was no "fit" for Fernandina, the third island Columbus visited, the theory was dismissed from serious consideration until 1985 when researchers collaborating with the American historian and map specialist Robert H. Power found credible solutions.

Grand Turk itself is an excellent fit of contemporary descriptions of the landfall. As in the rival theories, there are weak points in the explanation of Columbus's route through the islands but its credibility depends less on supposed errors in the log. Grand Turk itself stands up to historical scrutiny at least as strongly as either San Salvador or Samana Cay and is increasingly gaining recognition as the probable landfall island of Guanahaní.

(Inset) Columbus claiming the New World for Spain on October 12, 1492. Called Guanahaní by the Indians who lived there, Columbus renamed the island San Salvador. (Below) Dr. Luís Coin and crew row ashore in a reenactment of Columbus's historic landing nearly five hundred years before.

trinkets to awed Indians. He bestowed the capes and bays of the island paradise with holy or royal names, formally took possession of new lands and left large wooden crosses in his track. As a navigator Columbus led a charmed life, avoiding disaster almost by miracle as he sailed headlong into some of the most difficult and perilous waters known (the name Bahama stems from the Spanish for shallow water). His ships were carried this way and that by currents, headed by contrary winds and drenched in torrential downpours. He sometimes followed the canoe route indicated by local Indians rather than the obvious course across open water, so his track through the maze of similar-looking islands is the despair of historians because it is impossible to reconstruct it with any certainty.

Sniffing the perfumed air as he proceeded from one brilliant landfall to the next, Columbus found it impossible to conceive that the luxuriant forests were not loaded with valuable spices, that the coral lagoons were not carpeted with pearls. As if writing a daily picture postcard to the queen, he expressed his delight in everything he saw. Approaching a cape, "so fair and sweet a smell of flowers" wafted out to his ship that it was "the sweetest thing in the world." The trees were the most beautiful he had seen, "as different from those in Spain as day from night." Some trees bore "fine wool" (probably kapok); cotton grew wild in the field "like roses."

Netting in the lagoons, his men caught "fish painted a thousand ways in brightest hues of blue, yellow and red." They speared a six-foot iguana whose flesh, barbecued on the beach, proved "white, soft and tasty." It rained hard and frequently, but "the nights were as mild as May in Andalusia." The songs of little birds were "so marvelous that no man could wish to leave." Turtles were captured as they crawled ashore to lay eggs. Three manatees grazing on seaweed, mistaken for mermaids, were not as beautiful as legend had painted them.

When natives fled at the approach of the "men from the sky," Columbus said he ordered his men to respect their possessions. In their huts, with thatched roofs pitched high like Moorish tents, he found string beds called *hamacas* which would soon spell comfort for sailors. He collected seeds of corn called *maiz* which would transform eating habits and trigger population explosions from China to Africa. He licked from his chin the golden juice of a pineapple and dined on a roasted root vegetable with a flavor of chestnuts, the sweet potato. "Your highnesses may believe," Columbus wrote, "that this land is the best and most fertile and temperate and level and goodly that there is in the world."

Columbus noted the commercial potential of a resin-exuding plant he mistook for the valuable mastic gum seen in Chios, as well as crude cinnamon and the fiery wild chili with which his men spiked their rations. He praised the docility of the defenseless natives also with a commercial eye, reporting them "fit to be ordered about and made to work." But he dismissed their custom of rolling certain dry leaves into cylinders called *tabacos*, then setting them alight and inhaling the smoke through their nostrils.

After two weeks and two days of nosing among low-lying coral

(Top) The Old World depicts the New. This illustration, and the three others shown here are taken from Ramusio's 1556 Navigationi *and* Viaggi, *one of the earliest published accounts of the New World. These native dugouts were called* canoas, *the origin of the modern word* canoe *and were paddled with what Columbus likened to "a thing like a baker's peel."*
(Above) Although the large native lizard, the iguana, looked unappetizing, its barbecued flesh turned out to be "white, soft and tasty."

(Top) Among the many discoveries Columbus made were a whole variety of new plants, among them maíz *or corn, tobacco and, shown here, the pineapple. (Above) The natives slept in string beds called* hamacas, *which were quickly adopted by European sailors for use on their ships.*

islands, the flotilla came upon the north coast of a land he called Juana, though the natives knew it as "Cuba." But Columbus was puzzled. Unaware of the currents that had slowed him during the two weeks before his San Salvador landfall, he thought he was much farther west. The mainland he expected to find would lie on a north-south axis, while this high and handsome country with its lofty blue ranges seemed to stretch endlessly between east and west.

Coasting along its fresh green shoreline, marking one beautiful harbor after another and mooring in rivers so clear and deep that the ships' topsides brushed the banks and were overhung with palms, Columbus headed westward for five days. This led him to think he had discovered an extension of the mainland. The coastline then began to trend toward the north, an effect enhanced by the local magnetic variation affecting his compasses. Columbus wrote later this was "contrary to my desires" and he decided to reverse his course. In light of later events, we can suppose that Columbus thought he was in the Yucatan area of Mexico and had overshot the island he was looking for.

First, as he was in a suitable harbor, Columbus ordered the ships careened. One at a time they were run ashore. When the tide left them high and dry their hulls were scraped of weed and barnacles and then coated with pitch. While this was going on, Luís de Torres, the interpreter, was dispatched with a couple of Indian guides and a seaman who was a veteran of the African trade to visit a "town" said to lie twelve leagues inland. The letter and cheap gifts they took suggest nothing more than an exploratory sidetrip on the pattern of Portuguese trade in Guinea to seek and establish trading links with local chiefs, but it is presented in the log as an extraordinary embassy: "[I had] to try and go to Grand Khan, who [I] thought was here or at the city of Cathay, which is the Grand Khan's, and is very great, according to what [I] was told before leaving Spain."

It is surely asking a lot to suppose that Columbus, beaching his ships on the muddy shore of a tropical river near a few thatched huts inhabited by naked people, imagined he was in the vicinity of an immense, populous and sophisticated capital. No celestial city was found, but Luís de Torres did understand from the Indians welcoming him to their village that on an island to the southeast he would find people gathering gold on the beach by candlelight and hammering it into bars.

When the fleet began to backtrack along its route, the friendly easterly winds were suddenly its enemy. Repeatedly the three ships angled far out to sea, then tacked toward the shore only to find they had made little progress. The *Santa María*, unlike the slim and nippy caravels, was not built for windward work, and Martín Alonso finally lost patience.

On Wednesday, November 21, the flotilla was about forty miles north of the Cuban coast and bashing into head seas. When the flagship threw about to begin another slog back to the mainland, the *Pinta* continued on. Perhaps her crew had prepared the lateen sails that were ideal for sailing to windward. If so, as dusk fell they were hoisted in place of the square sails and the caravel cut away to the east, zigzagging more efficiently into the wind's eye. Martín Alonso's brother in the *Niña* did not follow, probably because Juan Niño, the caravel's owner and master, supported by his brother who was a crewman, had faith in Columbus. (They were later rewarded handsomely for their loyalty.)

Columbus was shaken by the desertion. He feared the *Pinta* would beat him to the gold and then race on to carry the news to Spain. But there was nothing he could do as he doggedly struggled eastward with his two remaining ships. In rare moments they were wafted along in balmy breezes. Most of the time they fought strong headwinds in torrential rain. Finally coming to the eastern end of Cuba, he started across the fifty-mile Windward Passage. To his surprise he now found another large and fertile island. He named it *La Spañola*, or *Española*—soon corrupted to Hispaniola, by which name it is known today (it is now shared by Haiti and the Dominican Republic)—and headed along its northern coast.

Christmas Eve found the two ships meandering in a calm sea off the high headland now known as Cap Haïtien. At last Columbus and his men were enjoying some hard-won peace. For three days they had been in a beautiful harbor where they had been deluged with natives who swam or paddled out in canoes. In exchange for trinkets, the Indians had given them pieces of gold along with calabashes of water and fish. Although Columbus makes no mention of it in the log, we can be sure the native hospitality included the sexual favors of their women, since this was commonly the case with these first friendly contacts. Columbus, as usual, had questioned several locals about the source of gold. Each one had gesticulated to the east and answered "Cibao...! Cibao...!"

Before he moved on, Columbus was visited by a deputation from a *cacique*, or high chief, whose name was Guanacagarí and who ruled over a town some miles east along the coast. The group brought a marvelous gift of a mask of hammered gold and pressed Columbus to visit. Since Columbus's ships were windbound, he sent a few men ahead in boats. They returned with glowing accounts of their welcome by thousands of Indians in a large town.

Before dawn on Monday, December 24, the ships shook out their sails to catch the breeze off the land. The day was hot and bright, the wind blew from first one direction, then another, and all were exhausted by the three days of native hospitality. As night fell Columbus decided not to stop to anchor. The wind was light, the route had been scouted by the boats, and Cibao, which is still the local name for the once gold-rich and mountainous hinterland of Hispaniola, lay tantalizingly within his grasp.

It was routine for Columbus to share the night watches with his officers. He himself took the first duty, Juan de la Cosa, the master,

took the middle and Peralonso Niño, the pilot, the third. Columbus's watch began quietly, and soon his head began to droop from fatigue. With the sea calm and the weather clear, he told one of his men to take charge and turned in. But that seaman, too, was worn out. Ignoring the standing order that no boy should be left in charge of the helm, he whistled up a young grommet to take over and stretched out for a nap.

Around midnight, about an hour after Juan de la Cosa should have begun his watch, the hapless boy felt a jarring vibration in the tiller. A swell broke around the ship in a smother of foam, the keel thudded into solid coral and the boy shouted in alarm. Columbus was first on deck. He ordered Juan de la Cosa to take the boat and run an anchor out astern so the *Santa María* could be hauled off the reef. At the same time he seems to have berated the master, blaming him for the mess they were in because it had happened after the beginning of his watch. If so, he was treating de la Cosa unfairly. It is an old rule of the sea that a man is not considered to be on watch until he has been called, and Juan de la Cosa seems not to have been called.

With charges of treachery and treason ringing in his ear— Columbus was accusing him of sinking his own ship—de la Cosa did not follow orders but rowed straight for the *Niña* lying half a

Contrary to the impression given in this late nineteenth-century print, the wreck of the Santa María *was the result of negligence, not rough weather, and the reef she hit was some four miles out from shore. On the night of the mishap the sea was calm with just a gentle swell, which pounded the hapless flagship on the reef.*

L. Adolf Gloss 1897.

league ahead. The caravel's captain refused to take him on board. Hard aground on a falling tide, the *Santa María* was pushed farther up the reef by breaking swells. In a desperate effort to lighten her, Columbus ordered the masts cut away, the water casks broached, and all but vital equipment slung over the side. However, as the tide dropped, the flagship lay over on her beam ends, coral heads punched holes in her planking and water poured in.

The news reached the chief Guanacagarí in his town four miles away. He immediately dispatched a fleet of canoes to lend a hand. Through Christmas Day, the stricken ship was stripped. The natives were not looters, and all provisions and gear were carried ashore to the chief's town where they were marshaled into huts guarded by his men. The native town that welcomed Columbus and his shipwrecked crew was situated on the flat shore of a small estuary and built around a big circular plaza with a well and the chief's huts at the center.

Columbus was mortified by the disaster. But he was consoled by Guanacagarí's assurances that he would find prodigious quantities of gold in nearby Cibao and mollified by banquets of rock lobster. In gratitude Columbus presented Guanacagarí with a shirt and gloves. His men demonstrated crossbows and steel-tipped arrows with which the Indians could defend themselves against raiding parties of Caribs who, marauding from islands to the south, ate their prisoners. In the midst of the partying, reports were heard of the *Pinta* lying farther along the coast, but a messenger sent by canoe did not find her, and Columbus would later discover that Martín Alonso had anchored up a river that lay ninety miles to the east.

Columbus put on a bold public face at his humiliating setback and persuaded himself that the shipwreck was providential. The diary glosses over his own negligence and puts the blame on Juan de la Cosa for his desertion and the people of Pálos for forcing him to take such a heavy and unsuitable ship.

The *Niña*, smallest of his fleet, was too little to carry everybody home. Columbus decided to build a fort which he named La Villa de Navidad in honor of the birth of Christ. There was no lack of volunteers from the two ships, and thirty-nine men were chosen to remain and collect gold until Columbus returned from Castile.

The fort was built on a sandy spit attached to the land by a narrow isthmus, where a river twists through mangroves at what is now a hamlet called Bord de Mer Limonade. Open to the breezes, it was mostly free of mosquitoes but was dry and covered with thorny undergrowth so water and provisions had to be brought by boat or canoes from the town half a mile across the river. It was a perfect site for a fort built on the traditional "curtain and keep" pattern. A channel was cut across the isthmus and barricaded with poles and brush to create a virtual island. On a defensive mound in the center was a simple blockhouse built with the flagship's timbers. The garrison was left with arms, provisions and seeds. Then the *Niña* took on wood, water, fruit and vegetables and at sunrise on Friday, January 4, 1493, the small ship set sail for Spain.

Although he was on the threshold of the goldfields he had been

A 1556 woodcut depicts natives gathering gold. The amounts of alluvial gold Columbus actually found were disappointingly small.

searching for, Columbus had decided that to continue exploring in a single ship, with no possibility of rescue in case of trouble, was simply too dangerous. Later that day, while sailing eastward along the coast, he sighted a high headland. Joined to the land by a low isthmus, it was the most northerly point of the island. It seems that Columbus recognized this conspicuous landmark without ever having seen it before. This is implied by the fact that he gave it a name of special significance: Monte Cristi, the Mount of Christ. He gave religious or royal names to almost everything he discovered, but why else would he have bestowed on a mere headland the most revered name of all?

Referring to the incident in his *History of the Indies*, Bartolomé de las Casas wrote: "This Monte Cristi [which] I have seen many times [and] is very prominent and resembles a heap of wheat...was on the edge of the mine of Cibao....It seems that it was divined in advance [by] Columbus." But soon there is even stronger circumstantial evidence that Columbus knew all along which landmarks would signpost him to the gold-rich area of Cibao.

As the *Niña* approached Monte Cristi, a seaman looking out for shoals from the masthead sighted a sail on the horizon. It was the *Pinta* surging down on the *Niña* with the breeze on her stern. The two caravels ran for a sheltered anchorage. A testimony given later in the *pleitos* described how Martín Alonso, after thrashing into headwinds for many days, had backtracked to the first of the Virgin Islands. From there, setting his course to the southwest as he had always urged Columbus, he had explored and claimed the north coast of Puerto Rico and continued on until, like Columbus, he recognized the landmark of Monte Cristi and found the region known as Cibao. That both had come independently to the same area by different routes argues strongly that they had learned of Cibao and its distinctive landmark from another source. It is hardly likely that the Indians, using only sign language, would have provided navigational information in such detail.

Columbus greeted the wayward captain with cold fury and an unholy argument ensued. Martín Alonso was unrepentant. He described his voyage and said that for sixteen days he had anchored in a nearby river, traveled into the interior and brought back alluvial gold. Half had been shared among his men and the remainder was for Columbus to give to the queen. But Columbus furiously refused the gold and ordered Martín Alonso to release the natives he had kidnapped.

What was said can be pieced together from two sources. Gonzalo Fernández de Oviedo heard from Vicente Yáñez Pinzón that Martín Alonso protested vehemently when he heard that Columbus had abandoned so many Christians with scant provisions so far from

Continued on page 176

Puerto de Monte Christi en la Isla eſpañola

From the description in his logbook, Columbus seems to have recognized the distinctive headland he named Monte Cristi, although supposedly no European had seen it before. Independently, Martín Alonso Pinzón arrived at the same place and found gold. An early artist's impression (inset) accurately shows the same contour visible in the modern photograph (below).

Spain, saying they would surely die. And according to Francisco Medel, the queen's representative in Pálos who was told of the argument by Martín Alonso on his deathbed, Columbus refused to recognize Martín Alonso's taking possession in the queen's name of the "heap of rocks" he had called San Juan (Puerto Rico) and stiffly reminded him that Columbus's powers were vested by the Crown itself. Martín Alonso promised to take the matter up in a court of justice on their return. "Then Columbus was very angry with him," Medel reported, "and said he would come and hang Martín Alonso in the doorway of his own house."

After Martín Alonso stormed back to his vessel, Columbus calmed down. Surrounded as he was by the Pinzón clique, he decided, according to his log, that it was not a prudent time to deal out punishment, and he grandly offered Martín Alonso his pardon. Then, after a brief scuffle with natives while trading for potatoes—the fleet's only unhappy encounter with the indigenous people during its ninety-six days in the New World—the race began to be first home with the news of their great discoveries. On Wednesday, January 16, the two surviving caravels set course for home.

The trade winds were now their enemy. Columbus's strategy was to angle northeastward from Hispaniola, close-hauled, until he hit the westerlies that would blow him toward Madeira. At first all went well. The days grew colder and the nights longer. An immense shark was caught, which helped to eke out their depleted provisions of hardtack, yams and wine. The *Pinta* sailed badly when hard on the wind because her mizzenmast had cracked. Two weeks out, the latitude of Bermuda was crossed, and they felt the first breaths of wind from the west. At long last the weary tack was at an end, and soon the westerlies were blowing hard. The ships now made tremendous runs of up to two hundred miles per day. Columbus must have expected the peaks of Madeira soon to lift over the horizon, but he had not reckoned on a storm of exceptional ferocity that hit them on Tuesday, February 12.

Under bare poles—"with dry tree" as it was quaintly put in medieval Spanish—the caravels scudded before a tempest of such power that Columbus blessed the staunch qualities of the *Niña*. With little weight in her hold the caravel rolled violently, and Columbus ordered empty barrels to be filled with seawater to steady her down. Both caravels took a pounding, with seas constantly breaking over their decks. The *Pinta* had to run farther off the wind than the *Niña* because of her damaged mast, but Columbus did not deviate from his course to stand by her when he could well have done so because he was to windward. For the second time on the voyage, Martín Alonso Pinzón and his caravel were abandoned, and they soon disappeared from view.

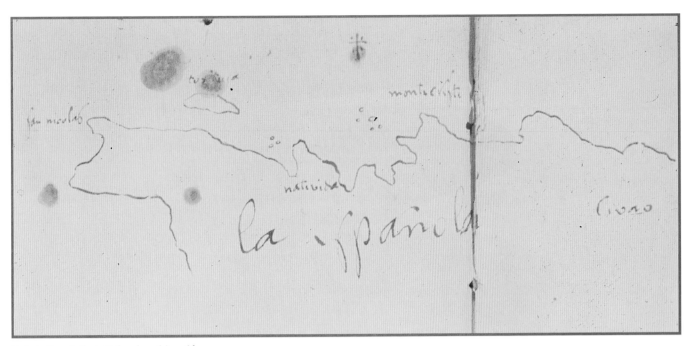

It is believed that Columbus himself drew this map of the north coast of Hispaniola, marking in Monte Cristi, and labeling Cibao.

In the *Niña* death seemed near. Three times lots were drawn to select men who would make Holy pilgrimages if God delivered them, and twice it was Columbus who drew the chickpea marked with a cross. Despite the fury of the weather, Columbus somehow dashed off an account of the voyage. This he wrapped securely in a waxed cloth that was sealed in a large barrel and cast into the sea, where it vanished forever. He did not want the record of his great accomplishments to go down with him. Then the world would never learn that he had been right.

By Friday the storm abated. Land was sighted, but it was three more days before Columbus brought the caravel to an exposed anchorage. Exhausted by lack of sleep, hunger and the first symptoms of the arthritis that would plague him for the rest of his life, he did not even know where he had landed. A handful of men who went ashore returned with chickens to stew, fresh bread and the news that the island was Santa Maria in the Portuguese islands of the Azores. The next day, as half the crew prayed in church to fulfill the vows they had made during the storm, Portuguese soldiers threw them into jail, charging that they had illegally sailed to the Guinea coast.

Before Columbus could intervene on their behalf, the gales resumed and the *Niña*'s anchors dragged. He was forced to abandon half his crew and sail from one island to the next in search of shelter. It was three days before he could return to argue for his men. With his logbook as evidence, he successfully convinced the local authorities that his ship had been nowhere near the Guinea coast, and his crew was released.

During the next leg of his voyage toward Spain, a squall split his sails, and another gale raged for four days. The wind was so strong that it seemed to lift the caravel into the air. Once again the crew made religious vows and drew lots that once again fell to Columbus. On Sunday, March 3, a lee shore of great cliffs was sighted, and it seemed the *Niña* would be driven to certain destruction. In a desperate bid to claw off, a scrap of sail was hoisted. At daybreak Columbus recognized the Rock of Sintra, a familiar landmark at the mouth of the River Tagus. Given little option in the matter, Columbus blew like a leaf straight into the port of Lisbon. "I escaped," he wrote, "by the greatest miracle in the world."

The *Niña* had escaped the storm only to find herself in the capital of the enemy Columbus had been trying to avoid all along. There followed a day of high tension when he was challenged by a sneering Bartholomew Dias, discoverer of the Cape of Good Hope, who now commanded the port's guardship. But finally his letters of authority from the Crown of Castile were recognized. As word got around that the Spaniards had been to the Indies, sightseers flocked to gaze at the battered caravel. Columbus himself was summoned to the monastery nine leagues inland where King John II was in residence.

It must have been a tense meeting for Columbus, but he undoubtedly felt a glow of satisfaction as the king received him with honor and graciously told him to be seated. According to the log, the king informed Columbus he was pleased the voyage had ended so favorably, but he understood from the treaty made earlier with Castile that the newly discovered lands must be his. Columbus indignantly responded that he had been ordered not to go near La Mina or any part of Guinea and he had not done so. The king listened to the story with courteous interest but he remained suspicious. Although he thought Columbus greatly exaggerated his accomplishments, John blamed himself for neglecting to back him earlier. When officials urged that Columbus be discreetly killed so his news would never reach Spain, the king demurred.

An easy two-day sail by way of Cape St. Vincent brought the *Niña* to the bar of Saltés just before sunrise on Friday, March 15. At noon she worked up the river on the flood tide and reached the port of Pálos from which she had sailed just eight months before. Word of her arrival had raced ahead, and the welcome was tremendous. Every man on board was a hero. With amazement and rejoicing, the four shivering Indians who had survived the trip were paraded ashore along with parrots, spears, plants and samples of gold the expedition had collected. Then, in the midst of the excitement, a second familiar sail was sighted. Incredibly, the *Pinta*, which had earlier been driven by the storms into the port of Bayona in northwest Spain, arrived home on the same tide.

Martín Alonso Pinzón was ailing and distressed. As he was helped ashore he exchanged no words with his triumphant leader. Assuming Columbus to have perished in the first storm, he had written to the sovereigns announcing "his" discoveries and requesting permission to come directly to Court. But news of Columbus's arrival in Lisbon had reached the monarchs before Pinzón's letter. Their reply was to warn Martín Alonso not to visit save in the admiral's company. Meanwhile, the rebellious captain was struck down by fever (or galloping syphilis) contracted while ashore in the Indies. Within a few days the one man who deserved to share the glory of the

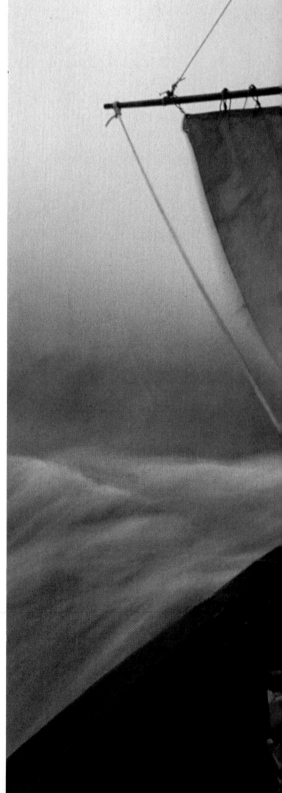

Rough weather aboard the new Niña. *On his homeward passage, Columbus encountered storms of such severity that he sealed an account of his voyage into a barrel and threw it overboard, in the hopes that, should he sink, word of his discoveries would reach the Old World.*

discovery was dead.

The triumph of Don Cristobál Colón, Admiral of the Ocean Sea, Governor and Viceroy of the Indies, was now absolute. Incandescent with self-righteousness, gleeful at the vast powers and riches that would be his, Columbus performed his vows in the churches at Moguer and Huelva. While staying at La Rábida he commenced planning a second, much larger expedition. Then he rode toward Barcelona where the Court of King Ferdinand and Queen Isabella were in temporary residence. It was a long ride of seven hundred miles. Columbus and his cavalcade probably joined in the Easter Holy Week celebrations in Seville, then tarried briefly in Córdoba where the admiral visited his mistress, Beatriz. Around the middle of April 1493, Columbus reached Barcelona.

For the Court it was a welcome diversion. Not long before, the king had been attacked and wounded by a man with a cutlass. At first it was thought to have been an attempted palace coup, but the assailant proved to be a peasant with a grievance. Still, the king and queen remained jittery. Now they had something to celebrate.

The approaching Columbus rode like a Roman conqueror at the head of an imperial procession. He was returning not only as a great navigator and discoverer, the victor over fearful unknowns, but as a seadog of courage, skill and unimpeachable judgment. The only conceivable parallel in modern times is the return of the first men on the moon.

Nobles and courtiers galloped on their chargers out of the gates to escort him through the packed streets in a display of splendor. First came the Indians, then sailors carrying live parrots in cages and a plethora of wonders such as the skin of the giant iguana, spears tipped with fish bones, skeins of cotton and bundles of wool that grew on trees, samples of spices, dyes and timber and finally chests containing the treasures—the mask of hammered gold, the gold bracelets and nose decorations, the purses of gold-dust. The sovereigns who awaited him on thrones beneath a canopy of embroidered gold rose to their feet as Columbus kissed their hands. He was accorded the priceless honor of being seated in their presence. The countenance of Christopher Columbus, as one biographer put it, beamed with modest satisfaction.

For the next month Columbus was the hero of the Court. He rode on horseback in the park alongside the king. All his titles, honors and privileges were confirmed. He was presented with 10,000 gold ducats (about $335,000 in today's money) as well as the pension of 10,000 maravedis for sighting land (some writers suggest that he gave this to Beatriz in Córdoba). His shield was emblazoned with the royal arms of Castile and Léon, an honor of inestimable social value.

Christopher Columbus had succeeded beyond his wildest dreams. With a single bold and majestic stroke of private enterprise, he had become a self-made grandee of Spain and secured his place in human history.

The new admiral would never again be so content, the world never again the same.

(Above) Columbus's personal crest displays the royal symbols of the lion of Léon and the castle of Castile, signs of the high honors Ferdinand and Isabella bestowed on him after his first voyage. (Right) Columbus was received at the court of Ferdinand and Isabella like a conquering hero. In this nineteenth-century painting by Deveria, he displays the bounty of the New World—gold trinkets and the natives he had brought back with him—before the monarchs.

COLUMBUS'S LEGACY TO THE INDIANS

When a handful of Arawak fishermen watched Christopher Columbus wade ashore at the head of his men and then drop to his knees on the sand to pray, two great branches of the human race at last came face to face.

Even as they joyfully welcomed the bearded "men from the sky" the natives—whom Columbus dubbed "Indians" because he thought he had arrived at a remote island outpost of the Indies—were unknowingly living out the last brief twilight of their existence.

The natives were Taínos, a sub-group of the Arawak culture occupying much of the Caribbean and the northern fringe of South America. Peaceful and gentle with only rudimentary weapons, the Taínos were being steadily routed by the fierce Caribs who were island-hopping the length of the West Indies, eating men and capturing women as they went.

Although the Taínos at his landfall were "so much our friends that it is a marvel," Columbus kidnapped six and shackled them to his deck.

(Above) Theodor de Bry's 1594 depiction of New World cannibals represents a distinctly European view of the inhabitants of the Caribbean. (Below) Columbus greeting the Indians on Guanahaní.

R.Holata   Outina.   R.Saturioa

He praised their docility while appraising their commercial potential. "They are completely defenseless and of no skill at arms," he reported, "and so they are fit to be ordered about and made to work, to sow and to do all else that may be needed...."

When the natives in the colony later founded on Hispaniola by Columbus fought back against the bands of headstrong soldiers and discontented colonists who terrorized them, Columbus punished the victims.

About 1,500 Arawaks were rounded up and the strongest shipped to Spain to be sold as slaves. Columbus decreed that every native had to produce a hawk's bell filled with gold dust every three months. Any native caught without a copper token to show that he had met his quota was tortured. Those who fled were hunted down with dogs. Thousands of natives were driven to escape the reign of terror by poisoning themselves.

According to some estimates, a third of the original 300,000 Tainos were dead within two years. In thirty years virtually every member of the gentle race first encountered by Columbus had been wiped out.

(Above) Contact between the Spaniards and the Indians quickly degenerate into open warfare as illustrated here by de Bry. (Below) To escape the cruelty of their Spanish overlords, thousands of Indians committed suicide as depicted in this illustration from Benzoni's 1572 History of the New World.

After his disastrous performance as governor, Columbus returned to Spain in disgrace as depicted in this late nineteenth-century painting by Lorenzo Delleari.

10 ADMIRAL OF THE MOSQUITOES

The Whirlwind and the Legacy

An oncoming waterspout is a terrible thing to see from the deck of a sailing ship. Draining the gutters of heaven, it twists down from a belly of black cloud and drills into the sea. The water is sucked aloft by the corkscrew of incredible wind until it seems that the ocean and sky are consummating an act of furiously destructive passion. A small wooden vessel caught in its path is annihilated.

Off the coast of Panama on December 13, 1502, ten years after the discovery that made Columbus the most famous mariner in Europe, a waterspout bore down on the four little ships under his command. Wracked with malaria, crippled by arthritis, suffering from gout and possibly syphilis, and by the standards of the day already an old man at fifty-one, the Admiral of the Ocean Sea, Viceroy and Governor of the Islands and Mainlands Therein was in a state of acute dementia.

As the twister approached in a fearful sheath of spray, the admiral mustered his crew and read from his Bible the passage in which Jesus, walking on water, bids his followers be calm with the words, "Be not afraid, it is I." Then, with drawn sword, Columbus feebly traced a cross in the sky and a circle around his feet. The waterspout, a devil exorcised, charged off in a new direction.

During this fourth and last voyage Columbus made no momentous discoveries but ended his seagoing career on a note of high-handed adventure. He had already battled for weeks along the coast of Central America against punishing head winds and in torrential rain—an amazing feat of endurance for a man his age. Two weeks after meeting the waterspout, off what is now Panama, he missed by just a few miles the chance to discover the Pacific. Instead he found a rich lode of gold at Veragua but his plans to mine it collapsed when a thousand natives attacked his stockade. When his ships were trapped upriver by a fall in water level, he fought his way out.

The two surviving vessels in which he limped onward, their timbers eaten by worms, leaked so badly that they slowly sank until their decks were awash. Unable to make it to the recently established capital of Santo Domingo on Hispaniola, Columbus beached them on the remote coast of Jamaica, where the ships' companies lived in thatched huts built on their decks. When he saw from his almanac that an eclipse would occur, he bamboozled the local natives with a demonstration of his powers to blot out the sun and frightened them into supplying him with the food and water he needed to survive. When half his men mutinied, he fought and won a battle on the beach. After nine months of fierce hardships he was rescued, but the ship he chartered to take him to Spain was dismasted in a storm.

The impressive fleet that embarked on the second voyage in 1493 consisted of seventeen ships carrying hundreds of expectant hidalgos *hungry for gold and conquest.*

On November 7, 1504, history's most famous sailor came ashore near Seville a scorned and pathetic figure destined never to comprehend the true value and scale of the new lands he had discovered. He had lost his friends at Court, and the queen herself was dying. Consumed by grievances and failing in health, for the next two years Columbus stumbled after the Court from city to city, pleading for audiences that were never granted. He failed to exorcise the vortex of controversy that, like some furious spectral waterspout, hounded him until the end of his days and pursued his memory down through the pages of history until the present.

He had sunk a long way. In 1493 Ferdinand and Isabella had lost no time in agreeing to back a second voyage. They also made an oblique reference to the neat trail of deliberate misinformation he had laid in his *Diario.* Columbus had given them a copy, but they wanted to know the whole story. In a letter dated September 5, just before he sailed from Cadiz in command of a fleet of seventeen ships, they asked him to reveal the true facts:

We ourselves and nobody else have seen the book you left us and the more we ponder it the more we recognize what a great thing this business of yours has been, and you have learned more than any human could know; pray God it will continue as it was begun.

And to better understand this book of yours, it is necessary to us to know the degrees at which lie the islands and lands which you touched and the degrees of the track you took; to serve us send them to us later. . .and if you think we should not show it to anybody, tell us.

The fleet set sail with fanfares and all flags flying on September 25, 1493, the ships packed with hundreds of adventurers eagerly anticipating the gold, compliant women and easy living in the tropical paradise Columbus had promised them. As the political zones

of the Atlantic had been redrawn, there were no enemy patrols to evade. A new agreement, approved by the Pope, had given Spain the western part of the Atlantic, while Portugal kept the eastern part. Even so, probably to preserve the secret of his route, the sealed instructions Columbus issued to his captains were to be opened only in the event that the ships were scattered; on arrival in Hispaniola they were collected again, unopened.

Although Columbus's own journal of the second voyage has disappeared, it is known from accounts written by others who sailed with him that after leaving Gomera he followed a course toward the Cape Verde Islands before turning west. This is perhaps the most obvious evidence that the route of his first voyage was also south. It is highly unlikely that Columbus would depart so radically from a route he had recently proved. In fact, on none of his subsequent voyages did he sail due west of the Canaries.

He did, however, head a little farther south than the path Dr. Coin had deduced for the first voyage. The reason for this is explained in the letter he wrote to Luís de Santangel just before arriving back from his first voyage—the same letter in which he stated that in twenty days he had reached the Indies. Since this letter was quickly printed and published all over Europe, it may be regarded with some confidence as exactly what Columbus wrote and the truest account that survives.

In the letter, Columbus observed that Hispaniola was in a good position for trade with the mainland not far away (to the west) and was close to the other mainland (to the south). Following the custom of Portuguese navigators, he disguised Hispaniola's true position, saying it lay 26 degrees north of the equator (actually it is 20 degrees), which he seems to have thought was close enough to the demarcation line of the latitude of the Canaries to avoid any quibbles from the Portuguese. This ruse may be one explanation for the fact that for two decades or more thereafter, maps plotted the New World 6 degrees too far north.

But his slightly more southerly route in 1493 had nothing to do with what he had found out during the first voyage. The letter to Santangel states that the island now known as Martinique was "the first island met on the way from Spain to the Indies." This is in fact the case, but how would Columbus have known it? Even if his first landfall in the New World was one of the Virgin Islands, at no point during his voyage did he come nearer than about 250 miles to Martinique. Although the natives may later have told him the island chain continued southward, he had no way of knowing which specific islands were closest to Spain. Yet on his second voyage Martinique seems to have been his destination. He could only have known this by way of information from another source.

It was an easy trip until, sixteen days out from Gomera, some of the ships were damaged by a fierce overnight storm. Then, due to the large number of passengers, water supplies ran low. "Being informed about those parts," one of them later reported, Columbus distributed nearly all the remaining water, saying that in three days he would show them "a new land and peaceful shores with glassy fountains and shining streams." Sure enough, three days later an island was sighted which he named Dominica. It is just north of Martinique. The crossing had taken twenty-two days.

As Samuel Eliot Morison pointed out, Columbus had taken his fleet to the very spot in the Antilles that is recommended in modern sailing directions for entering the Caribbean, although he had never been to that part of it. From there, he did not take the direct route to Hispaniola but hopped along the undiscovered chain of islands, first north, then west, many of which are out of sight of one another. The passengers were astonished at his uncanny ability to find one beautiful island after another, but Columbus had yet more tricks in store. "My lords," he said, "I want to conduct you to a place where one of the three magic kings live, who came to adore Christ, a place called Saba." Soon afterward the fleet arrived at a small island where Columbus asked a native what the place was called and was told "Sobo." It was the same word, Columbus maintained, but the man did not pronounce it correctly.

Some historians think Columbus must have learned about these islands from his discussions in sign language with Indians whom he met on his first voyage. But the natives had no written language, maps or compasses. Even if Columbus had managed to converse about such abstract geography as the disposition of islands some four hundred miles distant, and if the natives had demonstrated it with beans or pebbles, it could hardly have permitted such precision of navigation by ships arriving from the far side of the Atlantic. Besides, the Taino Indians could have known of the islands only from hearsay, because they were then in the hands of the fierce cannibal marauders called Caribs, of whom they lived in mortal terror.

Then, even more curiously, Columbus made an extraordinary find on the island of Guadeloupe. In a native hut was an iron pot and the sternpost of a European ship, too heavy and distant to be that of the wrecked *Santa María*. All who saw it thought it could only have come from the Canaries, proof that at least one ship had made it across the Atlantic before Columbus.

Leading his fleet proudly along the north coast of Hispaniola, Columbus sighted Monte Cristi and turned toward La Navidad confident of a joyful welcome from the men left behind. Instead he found a catastrophe, just as Martín Alonso Pinzón had predicted. All thirty-nine men were dead, evidently hunted down and slain by natives who could stomach no more Christian "goodwill" in the form of rape and forced labor. Some bodies found on the beach had had their eyes put out. From this moment, misfortune closed in on Columbus and dogged him to his grave.

But to hold Columbus accountable for the chain of disasters that followed would be to overlook the essence of the man. He was at bottom a simple seafarer of unusual curiosity, vision and ambition but of indifferent education, questionable leadership qualities and no administrative experience. His power resulted from a single voyage during which many of his shortcomings as a leader were manifest and almost defeated him. Now, setting up a colony in an alien land, he was expected to cope with problems that ranged from

La Navidad, the first European settlement in the New World, was razed by angry natives and its thirty-nine Spanish occupants killed, as depicted in this sixteenth-century print.

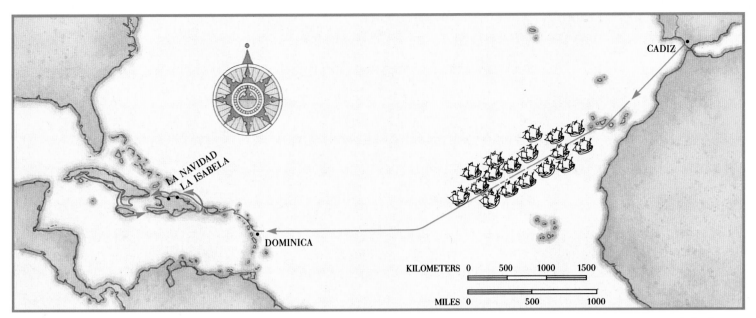

Columbus's second voyage in 1493 followed a southerly route that is close to the one Dr. Coin believes he took on his first voyage. Columbus predicted his landfall on Dominica three days before the island was sighted, although he had not been within 250 miles of it in 1492.

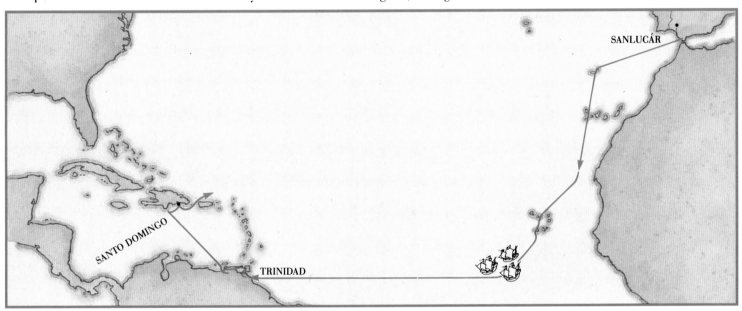

The third voyage, which left Spain in May 1498, touched the northern tip of South America, making Columbus the first European since the time of the Vikings to set foot on the mainland of the western hemisphere.

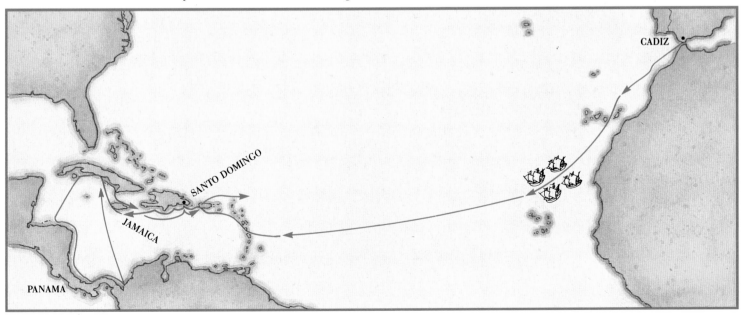

On his fourth and final voyage, departing in 1502, Columbus explored the isthmus of Panama, searching in vain for an open channel that would lead to the Orient.

town planning and gold mining to civil defense. As well, the majority of his twelve hundred colonists were prickly and headstrong *hidalgos*. He was out of his depth.

Columbus got off on the wrong foot by siting his settlement, which he called Isabella, at a foul and ill-watered spot with poor shelter for the ships. Its only merit seems to have been proximity to the goldfields of Cibao that he was in a fever to exploit. Yet the Rio de Gracía, where the *Pinta* had lain in safety for sixteen days, was only nine miles to the east, and there were even better harbors a little farther on.

Columbus evidently had in mind a contented and stable little trading colony on the Genoese pattern, but he found himself in charge of a nursery of conquistadors. Spaniards lived to fight, not engage in commerce or plant crops. Conditioned by their own recent tradition of reconquest, they knew only the doctrine of constant military advance and sharing of spoils. The admiral had led them to believe they would live like lords with docile natives tilling their crops and bringing them fistfuls of gold. Instead they lived in miserable conditions, facing hostile Indians.

One of Columbus's first acts was to build a fort in the hinterland of Cibao as a base for mining, but the gold was meager, and the alluvial deposits were soon worked out. The seeds brought from Spain, planted by the gentlemen adventurers who were reluctant to exchange their swords for shovels, did not flourish. Many of the settlers died of tropical diseases. Quickly the *hidalgos* became impatient and quarrelsome. Before long, gangs of soldiers and discontented colonists rampaged over the island terrorizing the natives. Unwisely, Columbus did not punish the mutineers but adopted the principle, as Morison put it, that Christians could do no wrong. Instead he punished the victims.

About fifteen hundred Taino Indians were rounded up and the strongest five hundred shipped to Spain to be sold as slaves. The governor decreed that every native man, woman and child over the age of fourteen should produce a hawk's bell filled with gold every three months. It was pay or perish. Those found without copper tokens to show their quotas had been filled were killed or brutally punished, while those who fled were hunted down by dogs. In despair, hundreds resorted to suicide by eating poisoned roots. Bartolomé de las Casas, who denounced the Spanish conquerers as bad patriots and worse Christians, described in his *History of the Indies* how natives were hanged in groups of thirteen "in memory of Our Redeemer and His twelve Apostles."

According to some estimates, about one-third of Hispaniola's original indigenous population of 300,000 was dead in the first two years, and within a few years of the Spaniards' arrival every member of the gentle subculture first encountered by Columbus had been wiped out. This left their islands so depleted of labor that black slaves were eventually shipped in from Africa by the million to toil in plantations. The process would continue for more than two and a half centuries, transforming the ethnic base of the Caribbean and the Americas.

*During his third stay in the Indies,
Columbus, facing open revolt by the
hidalgos he was supposed to govern, was
arrested and sent home to Spain in
chains. In this 1594 illustration by
Theodor de Bry he is seen being appre-
hended and relieved of his sword.*

Meanwhile, the admiral's administrative difficulties were not
aided by the fact that he was frequently absent on exploration—a
business with which he was more at home. From April to September in 1494, with the *Niña* as his flagship, Columbus explored to
the west. He discovered and sailed around most of Jamaica. Nosing
along the southern coast of Cuba, he saw that it hooked toward the
south and finally (an effect heightened by the magnetic variation
affecting his compass) to the southeast. Curiously, although nobody
is known to have discovered it before that time, the maps published
a few years later showed the existence of the Gulf of Mexico. It was
charted as a relatively small bay, roughly comparable in size with
the distances Columbus had sailed along the curving shore of Cuba.
If Columbus knew the gulf existed, it might account for his belief
that Cuba was the "*terra firma del poniente*," or mainland of the
west; had he sailed about fifty miles farther, he would have seen
it was an island.

After fighting against terrible weather and damaging the *Niña*
on a reef, Columbus returned, gravely ill, to Isabella. He was greeted by his brother Bartolomeo who had heard of the discovery while
in France and had followed his brother to the New World. Beset by
unruly settlers, sickness and other problems, the admiral decided
to abandon Isabella and establish a new city at what is now Santo
Domingo, on the south shore of Hispaniola. Then, needing to protect

Continued on page 194

THE FIRST EUROPEAN TOWN IN THE AMERICAS

Columbus's first decision as governor of the Indies was disastrous. He chose to site his first settlement on the open northern coast of Hispaniola, probably because it was nearer to the gold-producing area of Cibao. The town, named La Isabela after the Queen of Castile, afforded no safe haven where ships could anchor in all weathers. Drinking water was difficult to obtain, the soil was hard to work and unproductive and the area was hot and infested with mosquitoes.

The quarrelsome Spaniards had been led to believe they would live like lords with docile natives tilling their crops and bringing them fistfuls of gold. Instead they faced hostile Indians and a miserable existence. Crops failed and many settlers died of swine fever and other diseases.

After just five years the first permanent European settlement in the New World was abandoned. The colonists moved across the island to a more favored spot on the south coast at Santo Domingo, now the capital of the Dominican Republic.

In an attempt to restore the site a few years ago, the Dominican government bulldozed the remaining ruins, along with the topsoil and

(Above) The graveyard at La Isabela. Dr. José M. Cruxent, a Venezuelan archaeologist working at the site, speculates that some of the bodies found here are too large to be Spaniards of Columbus's time, and may be the remains of Guanches from the Canary Islands, perhaps pressed into service as soldiers.

(Below) A 1534 map of Hispaniola showing the location of La Isabela in the north of that island.
(Below right) A period woodcut of the construction of La Isabela, included by Columbus in a letter he wrote to Ferdinand and Isabella detailing the construction of the town.

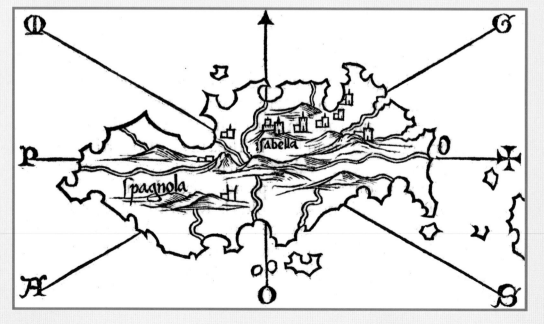

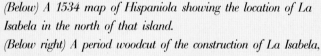

(Above) White stones mark the foundations of the town's buildings. La Isabela was laid out as a fort along very precise lines, with each building of approximately the same size.

(Left) Finds from La Isabela include the handle of a piece of pottery brought from the Old World, along with a horseshoe and a bent nail, both probably made on the site.

countless artifacts, into the sea. Teams of archaeologists painstakingly uncovering what remains of Columbus's first town, have discovered two main sections just over a mile apart.

The first houses were probably built near the bank of a small river where the ships unloaded. Later a kiln was constructed for manufacturing bricks and roof-tiles from clay found on the spot. Pieces of pottery made in the Spanish-Moorish style have also been found. It seems the settlers at first lived on little but shellfish. The small port grew into a farming center with limestone for building quarried not far away.

Later, a fortified part of the town was built on a wooded headland or "well-situated rock" where it could be easily defended against Indian attack. There was a church, a large storehouse or barracks 120 feet long, two prisons and about forty identical houses, many of them built around a central plaza.

The largest house, twenty feet by thirteen and built of solid limestone blocks packed with dirt, was no doubt that in which Columbus lived. Archaeologists have discovered that the house was protected by a stone wall where sentries probably guarded the unpopular governor against attacks from his own people.

his interests at Court, he sailed for Spain in the *Niña* and after a slow voyage arrived in Cadiz on June 11, 1496.

The new colonies were proving to be more of a liability than the treasure trove Columbus had promised, and it was two years before he was able to sail on his third voyage. Leaving on May 30, 1498, Columbus sailed directly for the "meridonial," or southern mainland he had mentioned earlier in his letter to Luís de Santangel. He named his landfall island Trinidad, then tracked along the Caribbean shore of South America. There, on a bony finger of land called the Paria Peninsula, now part of Venezuela, he was the first European known to have set foot on the American mainland since Norsemen landed in Nova Scotia five centuries before. Columbus recognized it as "a very large continent which until now has remained unknown." Nearly blind and constantly ill, he headed for Santo Domingo.

Columbus arrived on the last day of August to find the natives in despair from their cruel exploitation, the disaffected Spaniards in revolt against his brother Bartolomeo (whom he had left in charge of the colony) and nearly one-third of them suffering from syphilis. The admiral's rambling, incoherent and evasive letters conveyed to the sovereigns the feeling, as Morison described it, that he was not the man he once had been. His influence was rapidly waning, and his sons Diego and Hernándo, pages at Court, were taunted with allegations that their illustrious father was admiral of nothing but mosquitoes. By 1500 his weak and injudicious government had led to such a fiasco that he was arrested and shipped home in chains. Although the charges were later dismissed, his powers were never reinstated.

Though querulous and increasingly senile, Columbus did not give up. Despite his fall from high office, he pestered the monarchs into commissioning a fourth voyage, this time to search the Panama coast for a strait which could lead directly to the Orient and enable Spain to head off the Portuguese who had already reached India by way of the Cape of Good Hope. On April 3, 1502, Columbus sailed with four ships on the voyage that he intended to be his crowning achievement. Crossing the Atlantic directly to Martinique in sixteen days, he rode out a hurricane that wrecked a Spanish fleet that had just left Santo Domingo for Spain. As already described, this fourth voyage was a failure. He found no strait, brought home no gold and lost all his ships.

In Valladolid on May 20, 1506, Columbus died, as his son Hernándo put it, "from gout and other ills, and from grief at seeing himself so fallen from his high estate." His failures as a colonizer and governor were so manifest, his claims so outrageous and the former friends and supporters over whom he had trampled grown so numerous that the glory of his original achievement had long been forgotten. His humble funeral more befitted his simple origins than his lofty aspirations, and it was ten years before any official mention was made of his passing.

But a whirlwind of controversy pursued him beyond the grave and continues to this day.

Columbus died in Valladolid on May 20, 1506, his passing largely unnoticed by a world that had already forgotten him.

THE MYSTERY OF COLUMBUS'S REMAINS

On May 20, 1506, Columbus died "from gout and other ills, and from grief at seeing himself so fallen from his high estate," as reported by his son Hernándo.

The funeral of Columbus was a humble one and he was buried in the grounds of a convent in Valladolid. It is said that his remains were ex-humed in 1513 and removed to Seville where they were interred in the cathedral to be joined two years later by those of his son Diego.

Around 1536, however, both bodies were transferred to the cathedral in Santo Domingo, now the capital of the Dominican Republic. According to some accounts, the bones went to Havana, Cuba, when control of Hispaniola passed to the French in 1796. A century later, after the war between the U.S. and Spain, they were sent back to Seville where they occupy an ornate tomb in the cathedral (right).

The government of the Dominican Republic, however, avers that the bones never left Santo Domingo. Today they are interred in a marble crypt ceremonially guarded by sailors (below) awaiting relocation in the new $3.5 billion "Columbus Lighthouse" being built to celebrate the 500th anniversary of the discovery. Its 146 spotlights are designed to project the shape of a cross high in the sky.

The last joke may lie with Columbus for there is no certain evidence that his remains ever left the grounds of the convent in Valladolid. It is possible that the world's greatest discoverer lies buried beneath a billiard hall in a café that now stands on the site of the old convent.

11 Tierra a la Vista!

The New Niña *Finds the New World*

Rolling down the trades in the wake of Christopher Columbus in June of 1990, we glimpsed life at sea in medieval times as if it were being lit by lightning flashes. The shrill crowing of the cock that startled the life out of the weary crew on watch just before dawn. The waves rising high on either side, looking at us with a watery eye before subsiding with a hiss and rumble, as every sunrise heralded another day of the same peaceful routine that has changed little over the centuries.

Around seven-thirty the cook's flamenco wail announced breakfast. Sprawled limply in the pitch-black hold, the six or seven crew due on watch at eight were shaken into bleary life. The worst part of the day was wriggling into clammy, salt-saturated clothes. Then the new watch took their pots and eating irons from the capstan where they hung, clanking like goats' bells. Clustered round the forehatch, they collected fried eggs, bacon and chunks of hard bread from the cook and ate while wedged into some corner of the lurching deck. When they had finished and started their four-hour spell of navigation, steering and lookout duties, the rest of us could eat.

Mornings were spent in maintenance and other chores. At noon came the main meal—two courses of plain and mainly authentic fare such as rice or bean soup followed by cheese and olives. Dozing in a patch of shade through the long hot afternoon, I would hear all the sounds Columbus had heard when his ship was going well: the rudder groaning like a haunted house; the plonk of a bucket being dropped over the side and the splash and thud as it was lifted on deck, then the squelching as somebody washed his clothes.

As the sun dipped toward the horizon, the off-watch sailors played dominoes or cards, then joined in a noisy singsong of Cadiz carnival songs. At sunset, after a *tortilla* or bowl of soup, we gathered on the poop to sing the *Salve Marinera*, a rousing traditional sailors'

The crew of the new Niña *comes ashore in the New World.*

hymn. Then the long night began, the only sound being the roar of our bow wave unfolding on either side. In the moonlight the caravel seemed like an old etching that had come to life. One night, humming to himself at his solitary lookout post in the bow, one of the crew summed up what we all felt when he told me, "I'm hungry, dirty and worn out—I just don't know why I feel so happy."

As our voyage continued we had good reason to be pleased. In keeping with Dr. Coin's reconstruction of Columbus's route, we enjoyed day after day of following winds with not one day of calm. And there were some extraordinary coincidences. We caught a tuna on the same day as Columbus, noticed the same freshness of the seawater in the area of upwelling southwest of the Canaries, watched a brilliant meteorite shoot across the heavens and explode in a flash of white and blue (though not on the same day) and observed oceanic species such as tropic birds when Columbus did. More significant, however, is what we did not see.

For ten straight days the only living creatures were flying fish, the occasional jellyfish and a turtle that brushed along our hull like a startled green rock. Where the surviving version of Columbus's log reported calms, headwinds, false landfalls, a succession of land and river birds and big flocks flying overhead, we saw only a single forlorn swallow. It was only when we were very close to the islands that we saw the frigate birds, boobies and other shore-based birds Columbus reported.

Our voyage, made nearly five centuries after the event, could prove only the plausibility of Dr. Coin's theory. However, as I sat in the shade of the swaying sail and pored over the stark inconsistencies and untruths in the log as we know it, the theory seemed not only daring and original but overwhelmingly convincing. When academics come to study and reinterpret its finer points it may well be further refined. But what Dr. Coin has provided is a simple, believable story that fits the nautical and historical facts. For this reason it smacks of fundamental truth.

As I have already described, the detective story began when Dr. Coin first noticed certain puzzling discrepancies in Columbus's log—details that simply didn't fit a nautical reality unchanged in five hundred years. The more Coin analyzed the logbook, the more he became convinced that it had been deliberately falsified. Finally he concluded that it had been doctored by several hands in three different stages.

First it was falsified by Columbus himself to conceal from the Portuguese the fact that he had not only sailed into their waters but also made his discoveries more than 350 miles inside their zone. This doctoring consisted mainly of recording false course directions (always due west from the Canaries) and falsifying the distances sailed each day. The double distance reckonings have always been a puzzle to historians because Columbus's "false" record of 2,918 miles is uncannily close to the exact 2,975-mile distance from the Canaries to his landfall by the direct route. On this track his "true" record of 3,515 miles would put him far to the west, toward Acapulco. The distance he would have sailed by the southerly route, however, is

A crew member shaves off twenty-two days of stubble after the Niña has made land. Close to hand, freshly caught fish are grilled over the fire.

The deck was kept wet with buckets of seawater so the planks would not shrink in the heat.

(Clockwise from top left.) A crewman, clad in simple cotton tunic similar to those worn by fifteenth-century sailors, splices a rope.

Like Columbus, the new Niña carried chickens and rabbits intended for the cooking pot. The chickens did end up on the menu, but after a vote by the crew, the rabbits were set free in the Canaries. Meals were eaten on deck, and were occasionally seasoned with a dash of Atlantic salt spray.

about 3,600 miles, which matches his true figures almost exactly.

Next the log was "dressed up" by Columbus's son Hernándo, or perhaps other members of the family, to boost the image of the discoverer. This included adding frequent references to Cathay (China), the Great Khan and Cipangu (Japan), even though Columbus could not have thought he was anywhere near these places. Hernándo may also have removed references to mutinies and other embarrassing episodes.

Finally, the log was scrambled by an unknown hand—perhaps a clever lawyer, but certainly no sailor. This is clear from the nautical impossibilities created when diary entries from the middle of the voyage were exchanged with entries from a later phase. The reason for this final act of fakery was a lawsuit.

It was not long after Columbus's death that the treasure of the New World began to flow, gilded galleons bringing as much as four tons of gold a year to Seville. The Spanish Crown's original investment in the first voyage of Columbus is said to have yielded a return of 1,733,000 percent. With vast sums at stake, Columbus's son Diego, who became governor of Hispaniola, sued the Crown for restitution of the hereditary financial rights to which he was entitled according to the contract his father had signed at Santa Fé in 1492.

In the legal pleadings, which continued intermittently well into the sixteenth century, the Crown's prosecutor adopted the tactic of attempting to show that Martín Alonso Pinzón, not Columbus, had been the true leader of the expedition. The Spanish captain had quelled the first mutiny, sighted the first land, been first to Hispaniola and found the first gold. The *Pinta* was presented as the pathfinder and true discoverer of the New World, with the flagship lumbering in her wake and the foreign commander as only the nominal head of the enterprise.

To counter this ploy the heirs of Columbus, who became linked by marriage with the powerful Alba family, had to prove the opposite. Both the copy of the *Diario* that was made available to Bartolomé de las Casas for his summary and the biography of Columbus written by his illegitimate son Hernándo portray Martín Alonso as a troublesome and impulsive captain of little skill, always dashing off and reporting land where none existed. It was Christopher Columbus, the capable commander steadfastly maintaining his course, who held the expedition together and was the first to sight real land.

The family did not win its case and eventually agreed to settle for recompense in the form of titles and estates, but Columbus's record of the first voyage was now hopelessly fudged, and it is this distorted picture that has come down to modern times.

Bartolomé de las Casas—a friend and colleague of Diego— seems to have been a willing conspirator in the falsification of the record. In his *History of the Indies* he says it was unjust that the Crown should snatch Columbus's status and privileges from his descendants and accuses the king's prosecutor of calling as witnesses "great rivals of the Admiral" and putting "impertinent questions, outside the boundaries of justice and reason, so as to cloud and muddy

The house in Santo Domingo where Columbus's son Diego lived while governor of Hispaniola.

this, Man's most illustrious deed in thousands of years.'' The doctored originals of the *Diario* were conveniently lost and only the summary survives.

Having accepted Columbus's more southerly track as the true one, Dr. Coin then asked himself why he would risk so much to venture into Portuguese waters and why he was so confident of the distance to be sailed. Coin concluded that the explorer would only have taken this dangerous and unexpected route if he were acting on private information. It was then that the legends about the unknown pilot and his chart began to seem worth more serious consideration than modern historians have given them. Dr. Coin noted that in the log Columbus mentions a chart three times. Was this a secret chart that told him how far south to sail, where to turn west and how soon to expect land?

The story of the chart was widely known and believed in Columbus's own time. Of sixty-six witnesses questioned during the legal hearing of 1512 on the subject of the practicalities of discovery—many of whom had sailed with Columbus—forty-four implied that the admiral either did not voyage without a map or could not have done so. A similar pattern is reflected in the hearings of 1535. Columbus was even complimented on the accuracy of his foreknowledge by the sovereigns. In a warm letter to him dated August 16, 1494, Ferdinand and Isabella wrote:

It seems to us that everything you told us at the beginning

(Right) Christopher Columbus as a family man, with his two sons, Diego and Hernando, from an anonymous engraving.

occidentalis

has antilhas del Rev

A portion of Cantino's map of 1502, which shows a penisula north of Cuba that is almost certainly Florida—some eleven years before its discovery.

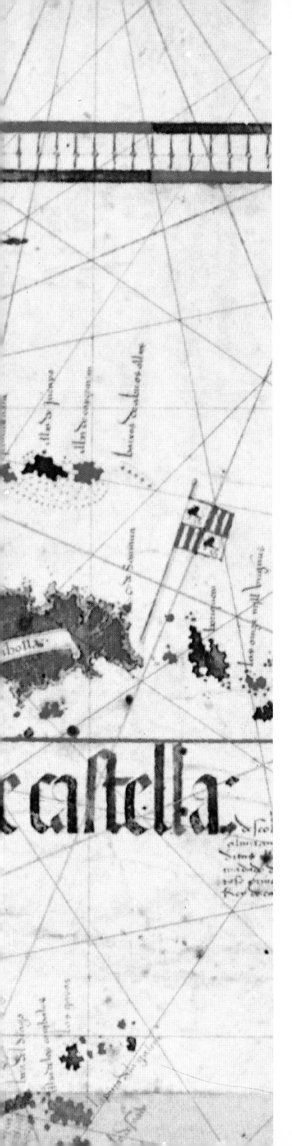

you could achieve has turned out for the most part to be true, as if you had seen it before you told us. . . .

As Dr. Coin considered the startling possibility, other clues, previously disregarded by historians, leapt into focus: the fact that Columbus knew from the start that he had to sail 750 leagues to find land and (when the figure is adjusted to the favorable currrent of which he was unaware) this is what he did; Columbus's uncannily accurate landfall on his second voyage at islands he had never visited; the various sly remarks of de las Casas in his *History of the Indies* implying that the admiral knew more than he was letting on; the remnants of a wrecked ship far from the spot where the *Santa María* had gone aground; and the suspicious way in which both Columbus and Martín Alonso seemed to recognize the headland of Monte Cristi on the north coast of Hispaniola though neither had seen it before, and the strange coincidence of their meeting there.

What if, he wondered, Columbus not only had a map, but that map depicted the headland that was the signpost to Cibao, where the natives were friendly and gold could be picked up off the ground? If he was looking for Cibao all along, no wonder he was apparently elated when he saw the headland and named it Monte Cristi. A chart would also explain Columbus's unbelievable success in navigating his way from one Carribean island to the next during his first and second voyages. And prior information would explain why he loaded the hold with cheap trinkets suitable for trading with primitive people.

Many historians persist in believing that Columbus thought the islands he discovered were close to Cathay and Cipangu. But he himself repeatedly referred to Cibao as being "at the extremity of the Indies." In one of his coy asides de las Casas wrote: "I do not know why he said in such a determined way that Cipangu was on the island [of Hispaniola]." In fact, if the name Cibao is substituted for many of the oriental place names appearing in the log, Columbus's account makes much more sense. He knew where he was going and he knew what to expect when he got there.

Some of the most interesting clues supporting the existence of a secret chart and suggesting what it might have looked like are found in the early maps of the New World. The first of these was made by Juan de la Cosa, the owner of the *Santa María*, who also accompanied Columbus on his second voyage. Perhaps to compensate him for the loss of his ship, Columbus taught him to make maps. Having copied all he could from the admiral's stock of information, the Biscayne captain set himself up as a chart maker in Puerto de Santa Maria and in 1500 published a map compiled from all he knew. Though added to since by unknown hands, this map shows parts of Central America and the Mexican Gulf that no navigator was

Continued

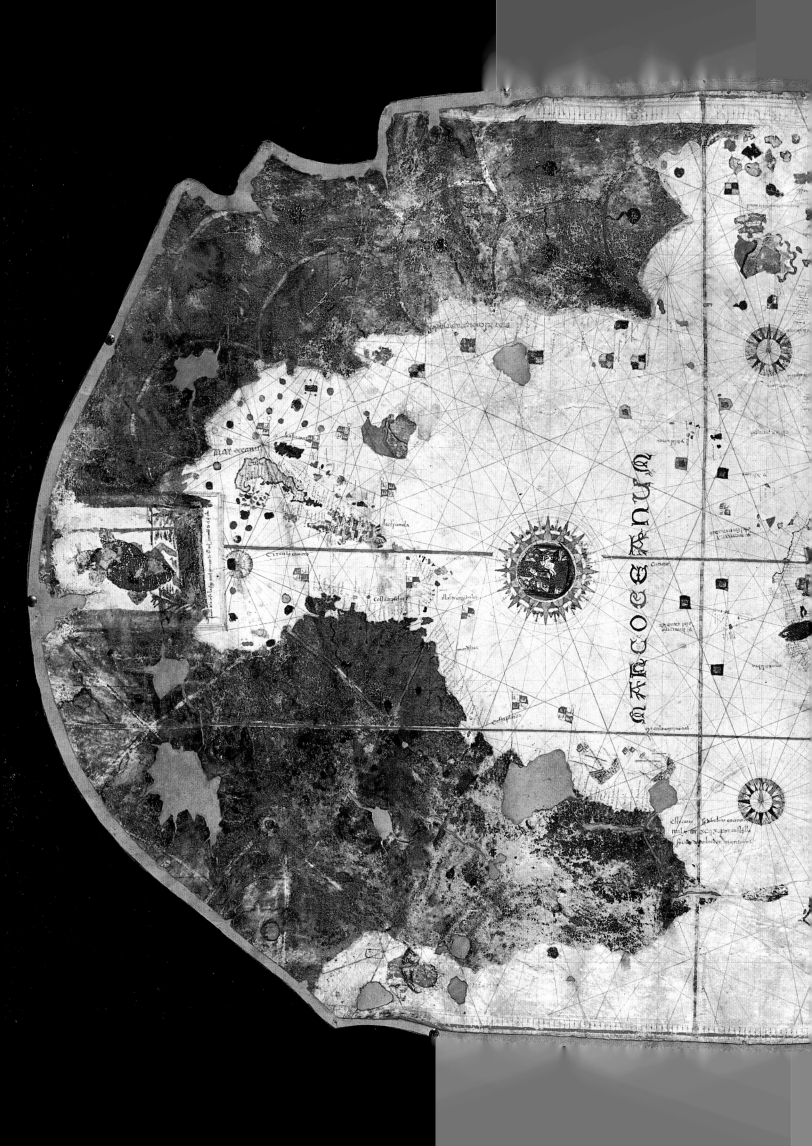

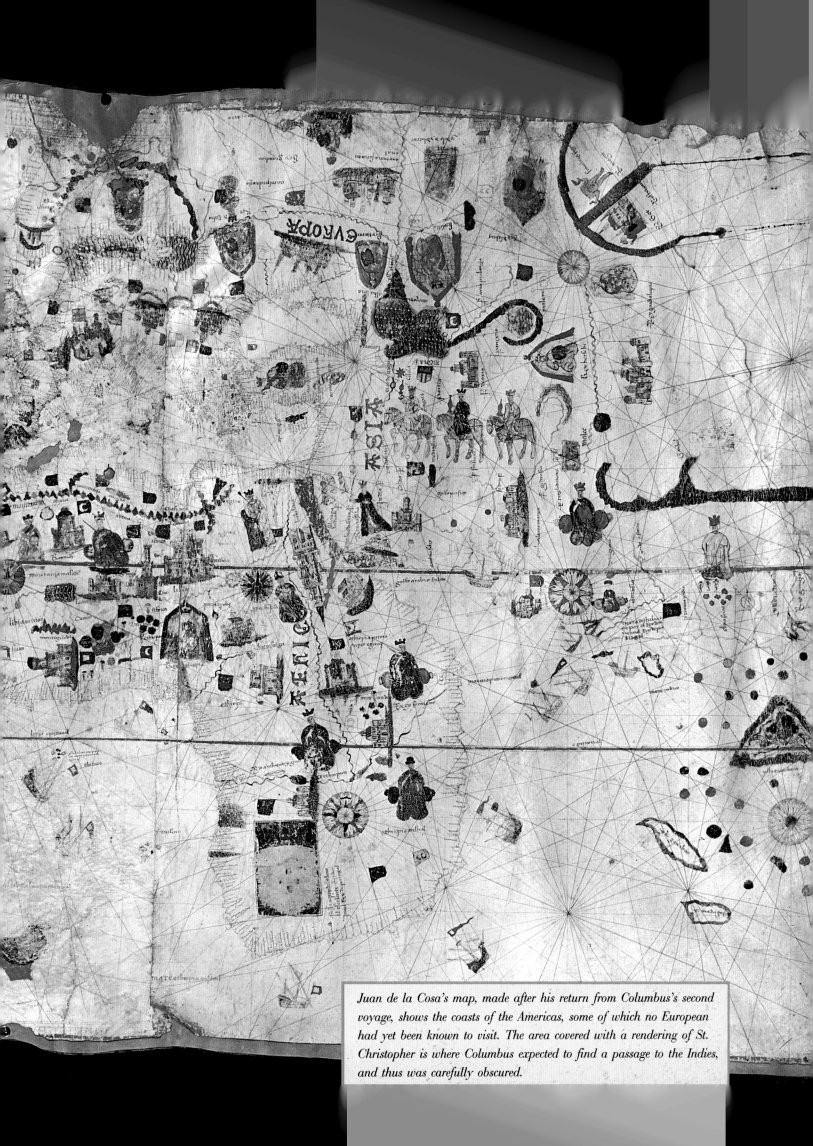

Juan de la Cosa's map, made after his return from Columbus's second voyage, shows the coasts of the Americas, some of which no European had yet been known to visit. The area covered with a rendering of St. Christopher is where Columbus expected to find a passage to the Indies, and thus was carefully obscured.

Within the map image: CHOR⁹, ZEPHIR⁹, CLAVDII PTHO ANDRINI, TERRA VLTERI INCOGNITA, PARIAS, SPAGNOLLA INSVLA, TOTA ISTA PROVINC, TERRA

known to have visited. Another map, copied by an Italian called Cantino from a chart smuggled out of Portugal and published in 1502, shows a peninsula suspiciously similar to Florida long before Juan Ponce de Léon discovered it in 1514. More compelling still is the large and important map made by Martin Waldseemüller and printed in 1507.

Waldseemüller was a German humanist and scholar who is believed to have begun work on the twelve large woodcut sheets in 1504, before Columbus returned from his fourth and last voyage. The map was based on two sources—Ptolemy and Amerigo Vespucci, who are credited on the published version in the form of portraits. Vespucci was a Florentine shipping agent in Seville who helped Columbus prepare ships for his third and fourth voyages. He himself made several exploratory voyages to the coast of South America and then was appointed to the sensitive post of superintendent pilot of the Casa de la Contratación in Seville. This was an agency of the Spanish Crown that compiled navigation information from the secret reports submitted by pilots returning from the Indies. Vespucci therefore had access to all Columbus's data.

Waldseemüller's map showed the Panama isthmus to be cut by a strait, something we know Columbus believed because he set out

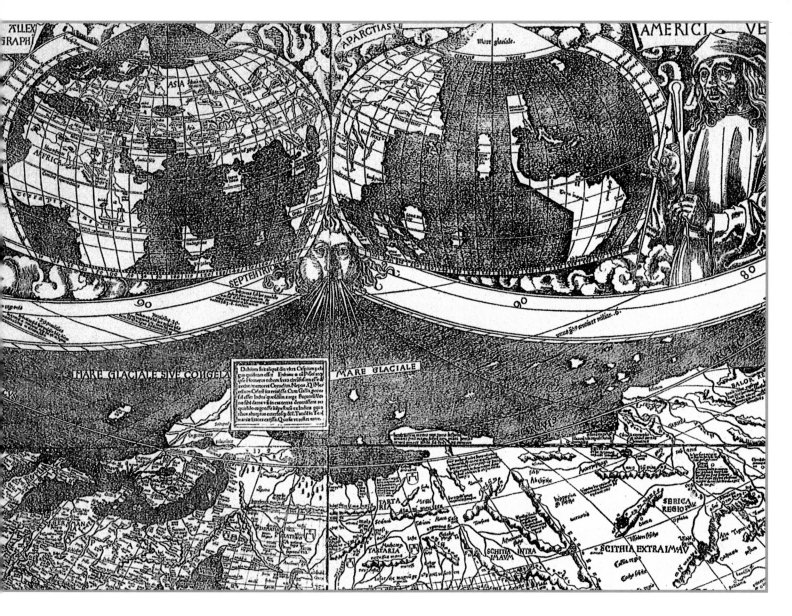

to find it. When he returned from his last voyage with the news that he had discovered no strait, the information reached the German too late for him to alter his intricate wooden printing blocks, so he incorporated the updated information in a decorative cameo. The main map, excluding Cuba (whose existence came as a surprise to Columbus) probably corresponds to the picture of the New World to which Columbus had access at the outset of his discovery voyage.

In sum, the evidence that Columbus set sail with some sort of secret information is very strong, though circumstantial. The most suggestive reference to it is in the logbook itself when, with a mutiny brewing, Columbus sends his "chart" across the water to Martín Alonso Pinzón. Very likely the original version of the diary contained more than the three references found in the summary, but these were likely removed when Hernándo doctored the record to burnish his father's reputation. Many puzzles in the Columbus story are solved if he had a map.

When Dr. Coin first spelled out the nautical evidence with which he had discredited the *Diario* of Columbus as we know it, I was impressed by the convincing simplicity and appealing logic of his argument. Now, scanning vast and empty horizons as day followed day, the winds invariably strong and on our stern, I was in effect staring the truth in the face. Our captain's painstaking reconstruction of events, supported by contemporary documents, seemed irresistible. In all the accounts I had read of Columbus he had remained a remote, almost legendary figure, but now my picture of him fell into place. In the light of Dr. Coin's compelling new theory, Columbus was no longer the unlikely visionary who conjured half a world from his imagination. I could see him giving orders from the poop of a ship like ours, sometimes tensely aloof, other times jocular, ever single-minded as he charged across the ocean—a seafaring adventurer staking all on a secret map leading him to gold, power and status.

His story was no longer confused by myth and mysticism. I saw Christopher Columbus as an accomplished and hard-nosed practical seafarer of evident curiosity, courage and charm whose career had lived up to neither his gifts nor his expectations. Then a fortuitous event changed his life. Columbus knew a stroke of luck when he saw one and had the nerve to pin his whole future on it. Over many years he patiently worked at acquiring the necessary sponsorship. He stuck out for what he wanted and when he got it he drove a hard bargain. By dint of sheer personal drive his bid for glory was successful. Despite unforgivable lapses in the loyalty he owed to those who sailed with him, his achievement was the epitome of private enterprise. It was only after the event when things went wrong and the records of his deeds were tampered with to suit ends other than his own that the truth became lost in the smoke of legal and political controversies.

The story as we now understand it goes beyond mere navigation, stripping away many of the enigmas that have confused and complicated the life of Columbus for so long. Explanations emerge for why he fled Portugal, why the queen changed her mind after interminably resisting his appeals, why Martín Alonso Pinzón supported him, why the Spanish captain repeatedly claimed to see land where none existed, and the real reason why two different distance figures appear each day during the outward leg of the voyage.

The real nature of Columbus's grand design comes into sharper focus. His inspiration is less baffling, his nerve and persistence in pressing his project on the monarchs of two countries more believable. We can understand how a solo entrepreneur could be fired by a single and tremendous idea, but what would account for the overweening confidence that impressed all he contacted, from the friars of La Rábida to powerful personages at Court and the queen herself? De las Casas reported that Columbus behaved "as if he had his knowledge under lock and key." Evidently he did.

Even if he did know where he was going and what he would find, it was Columbus alone who had the vision and strength of purpose to nurture his project for so many years. The lands he found were not only unknown to Europeans but were wholly unsuspected. To stumble over unknown bits of land by chance and lose them again, as the Vikings had done when they landed in North America five hundred years before, was only an incident in history. It took seamanship and courage of quite another order to turn the bows

(Above) Dr. Coin and his crew reenacting the landing of Columbus. The cross represents Christianity, the gibbet, the harsh justice of the time—the Spanish legacy to the Indies in a nutshell.

(Below) The story of Columbus and the egg, which became part of the folklore surrounding the famous discoverer, is here depicted in a work by the English artist William Hogarth.

of a ship deliberately toward an unknown horizon. Columbus had set out to find certain lands, found them where he expected, brought the news home and found them again the following year. This fact changed the course of human affairs. The glory of Columbus, as Victor Hugo notes, lies not in his having arrived but in having weighed anchor. This was the spirit that unveiled the Americas.

As more and more ships crossed the Atlantic, and the open ocean quickly lost its terror, Columbus is said to have been taunted at a banquet with the accusation that anybody could have done what he did. In answer, the story goes, Columbus passed a boiled egg around the table and challenged anybody to stand it upright. No one could do so until Columbus tapped the egg on the table to flatten part of its shell, neatly underscoring the point that a deed looks easy after it has been demonstrated.

For us, sailing in his wake, the discomforts of voyaging in the medieval manner were exhausting, even though we knew from our navigation by sextant precisely where we were on the chart. After twenty days, slowed by heavy swells and our escorting yacht, we were still about two hundred miles from the small islands outlying the northern end of the West Indies where Martín Alonso Pinzón first saw land. The faces of our crew were grizzled and deeply tanned by sun and wind. The big main yard creaked over our heads as it had done ceaselessly through 2,500 miles of sailing so far. Much of the tar had worn off the bulwarks and topsides so the caravel had a faded, weatherworn look. Looking about me at the bearded faces, sun-bleached ropes and stained sails, I would never have guessed that nearly five centuries had elapsed since Christopher Columbus first passed this way.

Now more and more birds flew around us. As heavy squalls raced up astern and lashed us with rain, we stood with our bodies soaped and ready for the blasts of blissfully cool, fresh water. But our food was running out, the hard bread soft and mouldy, the eggs gone. For the last week we had only one hot course a day, usually sticky rice with a sliver of blood sausage. On the twenty-first day I helped to cook the last spaghetti, serving it up with most of our remaining garlic, leaving only flour and water in the stores.

That black and rainy evening Alfredo, a hungry but resourceful crew member, contrived a pastry gun by enlarging a medical syringe with his sheath knife and lashing it with string to the end of a trouser leg he had cut from his jeans. Up before dawn, he used the makeshift gun to inject strips of dough into a pan of boiling oil and produced a heap of tasty *churros*, those wriggly strips of fried doughnut sprinkled with sugar that constitute a traditional Spanish breakfast. During the night we had sailed within eight miles of the island of Barbuda without seeing it. Now we were inside the Caribbean, but the horizon was thick with rain. Then, looking out from the *Niña's* poop, Alfredo earned the thousand-dollar reward by spotting the faint outline of the twin peaks of St. Bartholomew, one of the Virgin Islands, about ten miles abeam.

"*Tierra a la vista...!* Land in sight...!"

In twenty-two days we had found the Indies.

THE SECRET MAP OF CHRISTOPHER COLUMBUS

If Christopher Columbus was guided to the Americas by a secret map, what could it have looked like?

Although the map itself will undoubtedly remain a secret forever, Dr. Coin believes some elements of what it showed can be inferred from Columbus's decisions and from other maps published before or soon after his death.

The first known map of the New World was drawn by Juan de la Cosa (see pages 206-207), owner and master of the *Santa María*. Mysteriously, it includes long stretches of the Venezuelan and Gulf of Mexico coastline which had not been explored before the map was published in 1500.

On his second voyage Columbus is known to have coached Juan de la Cosa in mapmaking skills, perhaps as compensation for the loss of his ship, but when de la Cosa later set himself up in business, Columbus furiously accused him of stealing his private information. The Caribbean section of this famous map could have been based at least in part on what Columbus knew.

Another puzzle of the de la Cosa map is the large image of St. Christopher covering Central America. As it seems to be the work of a different hand and added later, what could it conceal?

Columbus believed that a strait existed in what is now Panama and in 1502 sailed on his fourth and final voyage to locate it. Direct access to the Orient would have been of immense value and the Spanish would have wanted to conceal any hint of it.

At about the same time, Martin Waldseemüller, a German cosmographer, began preparing the twelve wooden printing blocks of a large new map (see pages 208-209). The two portraits in the

This map reconstructs the main elements of information Columbus might have held in his hand when he sailed from Spain in 1492. The hypothetical route of the unknown pilot is also outlined. (1) Driven by a hurricane, the unknown ship reaches the Caribbean near the 19th or 20th parallel. The ship's pilot, making a chart as he goes, learns about the disposition of islands from the natives. (2) Exploring along the chain of islands, it reaches a place they call Cibao. (3) Heading southward, the pilot judges that the island now known as Martinique is the most easterly. (4) The ship coasts along the shore of Venezuela and Columbia. (5) Near what is now Panama, the pilot hears of a canoe route to another sea. (6) By now many of the crew are sick and the ship's timbers riddled with worms. (7) Struggling to survive, the pilot sets a course for home. (8) Near the tip of Florida, the pilot guesses at the extent of the Gulf of Mexico and misses Cuba but assumes the signs of land toward the east to be islands. (9) Fighting head-winds, the ship is carried among the Bahama islands and then struggles into the open Atlantic.

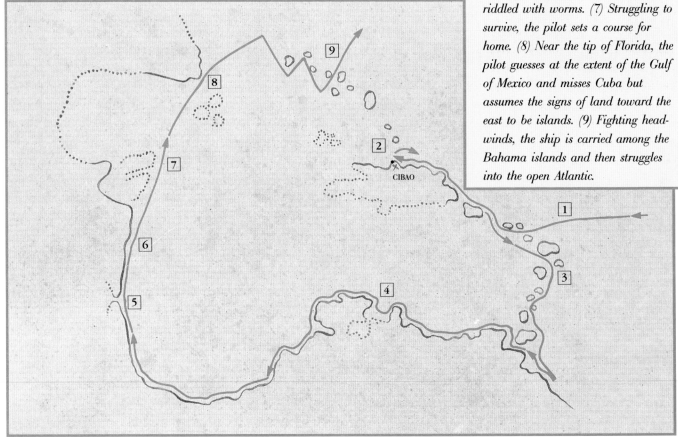

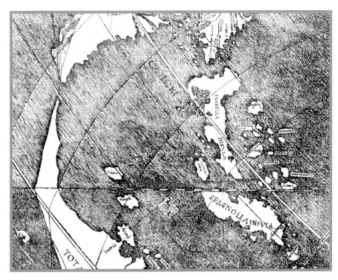

The Caribbean area of the map drawn by Juan de la Cosa includes stretches of the Venezuela/Columbia coastline as well as the tip of Florida which were not known to have been discovered when it was published in 1500. The mapmaker was accused of stealing Columbus's private material.

This area of the map drawn by Martin Waldseemüller depicts the area which, on the Juan de la Cosa map, is concealed by the image of St. Christopher. Columbus set out in 1502 to locate the strait. Waldseemüller seems to have had access to the same information as Columbus.

decorative frieze acknowledge his sources. Europe, Asia and Africa were taken from the work of Ptolemy while the New World was drawn from information provided by Amerigo Vespucci. For the first time the name America appears, on what is now Brazil.

A friend of Columbus, Vespucci was a Florentine who sailed on several voyages to South America. When he became chief of the Spanish Crown's pilotage agency, which assembled navigation data and prepared charts of the New World, there is evidence that Vespucci was admonished for releasing information to foreigners.

In 1504 Columbus returned to Spain and word reached Waldseemüller that no strait had been found. It was apparently too late to change the printing blocks of the main map so he incorporated a smaller amended version next to Vespucci's portrait. Dr. Coin theorizes that the depiction of Central America in the main map could well have been based on Columbus's secret information which was passed to Waldseemüller by Vespucci.

That the Gulf of Mexico is represented almost identically on the Juan de la Cosa and Waldseemüller maps, although it was not explored until 1506, supports the view that both maps were based on Columbus's original information.

Columbus seems to have confused the island of Cuba with either the Yucatan or Florida peninsulas, which suggests that Cuba was not shown on his map. The Cantino map (see pages 204-205) of 1501-2 also shows what could well have been Florida though it was not known to have been discovered at the time.

On the premise of an approximated and highly speculative depiction of what the unknown pilot might have given Columbus before he died in his house, one could hazard the likely route of a ship inadvertently blown across the Atlantic by a hurricane.

Having survived the storm, the Portuguese ship did not head directly for home. Sketching and surveying with crude instruments as he explored, the ship's pilot made a rough overall map of the West Indies which included a large island with a distinctive headland on its northern tip signposting an area called Cibao, whose friendly and unarmed natives readily exchanged gold for

baubles. He would also have kept a "pilot book" in which he sketched and described in detail scores of anchorages and landmarks.

The ship perhaps back-tracked to the coast of Venezuela then explored Central America. In Panama it is easy to imagine the pilot understanding by sign language that a passage led across to another ocean, though it turned out to be a chain of lakes accessible only to the natives' small boats.

With its men suffering from syphilis and tropical diseases and its timbers riddled with worms, the ship set course for home sailing northwards from Panama. There was now little time to explore, and possibly the pilot's skills were deteriorating. The pilot was vague about the Gulf of Honduras while the Gulf of Mexico was identified but its extent could only be estimated. The western tip of Cuba was plotted as only a few sketchy islands, and the ship made its final departure from Florida.

If Columbus did have a map in his hand when he discovered the New World, much of his confusion could stem from the fact that he was trying to force the map to fit the landmarks he found.

A COLUMBUS CHRONOLOGY

1451: The most likely date of Columbus's birth. Columbus is born in Genoa, son of Susanna and Domenico Colombo, a weaver then serving as one of the keepers of the city's gates.

1465: Columbus first goes to sea, probably on short runs down the Italian coast or voyages to Corsica at first, then broadens his experience as a merchant sailor.

1474-1475: Columbus journeys to Chios, a Genoese-controlled island threatened by the Ottomans at the eastern end of the Mediterranean.

August 1476: Columbus ships out from Noli as a crewmember in a fleet of merchant ships headed for Lisbon, England and Flanders. Off Cape St. Vincent, they are attacked by French and Portuguese privateers. Columbus's ship is sunk and he washes ashore near Lagos in Portugal. From there, he heads for Lisbon.

Autumn 1477: After only a few weeks in Lisbon, Columbus ships out again, this time in a ship bound for Southampton in England. From the English port of Bristol, Columbus may have sailed to Iceland and perhaps even as far north as Jan Mayen Island, above the Arctic Circle.

1478-1484: During these years, perhaps while living on Porto Santo, Columbus gets his idea of sailing west to find the Indies, the product of either his questing imagination, or a lucky piece of information, perhaps a secret map.

Fall 1479: Columbus marries Felipa Moniz Perestrello, daughter of the first hereditary governor of Porto Santo. Columbus and Felipa move to Porto Santo after the wedding.

1481: Columbus probably sails to the Portuguese trading fort of La Mina, in Guinea. In five years, he has sailed to the limits of the known world.

1484: Columbus approaches King John II of Portugal with his plan for an expedition to seek lands to the west. A body of experts convened by King John declares the idea impractical.

Autumn 1484: Columbus, with his son Diego, arrives at Pálos in Spain. On landing, he makes his way to the monastery at La Rábida where he meets the prior, Fray Antonio de Marchena, whose interest in science has earned him the nickname the astronomer priest.

1485: The Duke of Medina Celi, one of Spain's wealthiest men, offers to sponsor Columbus. The plan collapses when, upon informing the Queen of his intentions, the Duke is told that exploration is the exclusive monopoly of the crown.

April-May 1486: Columbus meets King Ferdinand and Queen Isabella for the first time.

1486-87: A committee appointed by Ferdinand and Isabella examines Columbus's ideas. The committee never formally makes its findings known, but Columbus senses they don't support him. Despite this, the Catholic Sovereigns continue to make periodic payments to him.

1491: Frustrated by neglect, Columbus considers looking for sponsorship outside Spain, in England or France. While visiting La Rábida, Columbus meets Fray Juan Pérez, the Queen's former confessor, who champions his case at court. For whatever reason, possibly because he has shown them the source of his information, Columbus is told the Catholic Sovereigns will consider his plan after the Moors are driven from Spain.

January 6, 1492: Ferdinand and Isabella take possession of Granada. Columbus enters the city with them.

April 17, 1492: Ferdinand and Isabella sign the Santa Fé document, outlining the privileges and profits Columbus can expect as a result of his discoveries.

August 3, 1492: Columbus and his three ships, the *Niña*, the *Pinta*, and the *Santa María*, leave Spain for the Canary Islands.

September 6, 1492: Columbus's ships depart from Gomera in the Canary Islands. After wallowing in calms for three days, his ships steer west to avoid a Portuguese war squadron. After one day, contrary to statements in his log, Columbus swings toward the Cape Verde Islands in the south. Later he turns west again and crosses the Atlantic on the 19th or 20th parallel.

September 25, 1492: "In twenty days I found the Indies." Columbus's men spot a low-lying island, probably Sombrero in the Virgin Islands group, only to lose it again.

October 12, 1492: After edging along the outer rim of Caribbean islands for nearly two weeks, Columbus goes ashore on Guanahaní, which he renames San Salvador.

October-November 1492: Columbus and his crews explore the Caribbean, threading their way between countless shoals and small islands. They sight Cuba, then swing eastwards.

December 1492: Columbus and his men reach the western end of Hispaniola, and moving east along its northern coast discover the headland he names Monte Cristi. Natives tell Columbus that Cibao, the source of much gold, is not far away.

December 25, 1492: The *Santa María* is wrecked on a reef off Hispaniola.

January 16, 1493: Columbus's surviving ships, the *Niña* and the *Pinta*, set course for home, having left behind 39 members of the expedition at La Navidad, the first European settlement in the New World.

March 4, 1493: After battling fierce Atlantic storms, and having some of his crew arrested in the Azores, Columbus sails up the Tagus to Lisbon. Columbus successfully convinces King John that he has not violated Portuguese waters.

March 15, 1493: Columbus arrives at Pálos. He proceeds overland to Barcelona, where he is given a hero's welcome by Ferdinand and Isabella. Columbus's power and influence are at their zenith.

September 25, 1493: Columbus departs from Cadiz on his second expedition to the New World with seventeen ships carrying hundreds of colonists.

November 27, 1493: Columbus hits the West Indies near present-day Dominica and heads for Hispaniola. There he discovers that the natives, goaded by Spanish mistreatment, have razed La Navidad and murdered all 39 of its inhabitants.

January 1494: Columbus founds a new settlement, Isabela, to the east of La Navidad. Columbus explores the coast of Cuba and discovers Jamaica.

March 1496: Columbus leaves the New World for Cadiz.

June 11, 1496: Columbus arrives home in Cadiz.

May 30, 1498: Columbus leaves Sanlucár on his third expedition.

July 31, 1498: Columbus arrives at Trinidad, then explores along the mainland of South America. Landing on what is now Venezuela's Paria Peninsula, he becomes the first European to set foot on the American mainland since the Vikings, five centuries before.

August 1500: Following a revolt by colonists on Hispaniola against the rule of his brother Bartholomew, Columbus is arrested, and shipped home in chains. He is soon freed.

April 3, 1502: Columbus departs on his fourth voyage. He explores along the coast of Panama, hunts for gold, and, his ships badly damaged by worm, spends several months stranded in Jamaica, where he puts down a mutiny and fends off angry natives.

November 1504: Columbus arrives home in Spain.

May 20, 1506: Columbus dies at Valladolid, surrounded by his sons and a few loyal friends. Nearly a decade will pass before any official notice is made of his death.

THE CREW OF THE *NIÑA*

AND HER ESCORT YACHT *TARTESSOS*

DURING THE ATLANTIC CROSSING,

JUNE-JULY 1990

José-Maria Anillo Muñoz
Miguel Angel Blasco Molina
José-Luis Cano Manuel Diaz
Alvaro Dusmet Garcia-Figueras
Antonio Gamera Aguirre
Gerardo Gantes Rodriguez
Ambrosio Garcia Vara
Juan Lijó Pereles
David Lopez Armario
Mata Majó Abella
Alfredo Martinez Vadillo
Luis Fernando Morillo Montañes
Mariano Muñez Fernandez
Carlos Platero Caraballo
Edouardo Presa Pereda
Pedro-Angel Puertas Rios
Manuel Suero Alonso
Rafael Vides Sanches
Fernanda Lazcano Pardo (doctor)
Carlos Yañez-Barnuevo Garcia (doctor)
Jose Sevilla Gutierrez (cook)
Juan Ignacio Liaño Ortuzar (cook)
Prof Juan Mantero Betanzos (mate, *Tartessos*)
Prof Carlos Suavez Escobar (captain, *Tartessos*)
Dr Luís Miguel Coin Cuenca (captain, *Niña*)

218

ACKNOWLEDGEMENTS

John Dyson and Peter Christopher would like to express their thanks to:

The University of Cadiz, whose cheerful and companionable students and teaching staff of the Nautical College drove the caravel *Niña* and her escort safely across the Atlantic, and Sr. José Luis Romero Palanco, Rector, for his support;

Captain Juan Landeta Bilbao and Captain José M. Spiegelberg, director and assistant director of the Nautical College, whose encouragement and support never flagged;

The Fundación Rafael Alberti, Diputación Provincial de Cadiz, owner of the caravel;

Barry Fox, chief executive of Fox Television Ltd of London, who staked the venture from the beginning, and his crew Peter Fox and Roy Page who brought the chocolate biscuits;

Captain Fernando Benítez, whose energy and determination hastened the preparation of the caravel to ensure we did not get caught by the hurricane season;

Trasatlantica Line, which allowed our two vessels to travel back to Cadiz in style, on the deck of a cargo ship;

Professor Juan M. Nieto Vales, who assisted enthusiastically in the preparations but at the last moment was prevented by illness from sailing with us;

Wm Harvey & Sons, who contributed toward the cost of new sails and provided a barrel of sherry for the voyage;

CRAME, of the Radio Holland Group, for contributing to the costs of an emergency radio beacon which was fortunately never required to prove its worth;

Dr. José-Maria Luzon, director of the Archeological Museum of Madrid, for his good advice;

Sr. Humberto Ybarra Coello de Portugal, of Hijos de Ybarra S.A., who stocked the *Niña* with potato crisps, vinegar, mayonnaise, salt and fine olive oil;

Sr. José-Tomás Carmona and Sr. Luis de Soto Ybarra, of The Association of Table Olive Exporters, in Seville, who provided more tasty olives than we could eat;

Sr. Juan de Castellvi, Vice-President of the Chamber of Commerce of Cadiz, whose advice and encouragement were invaluable;

The brothers Valeriano and José-Maria Sanchez Sandoval, of the Guadelete Boatyard in Puerto de Santa Maria, and their workers, whose skills and craftsmanship ensured we stayed afloat;

Captain Rafael Lobeto, director-general of the Merchant Marine of Spain, for his support;

Porto Sherry Marina, for berthing the *Niña*.

Madison Press Books would like to thank: Sabine Oppenländer, of Sabine Oppenländer Associates, and Ancilla Antonini, of INDEX, for their assistance in locating many of the pictures used in this book; Ute Körner and Lora Fountain who also tracked down and ordered hard-to-find pictures; Captain Ernst E. Cummings, of the United States Coast Guard, and Mensun Bound of Oxford University, who read the manuscript and offered us their comments; Catherine Marjoribanks, for proofreading the manuscript, and Martin Dowding, for compiling the index.

ILLUSTRATION CREDITS

All color photographs, unless otherwise designated, are by Peter Christopher © 1990.

Front flap: Columbus portrait, Arxiu MAS, Barcelona.

Back cover: (Top) *12.X.1492* by Antonio Brugada. Museo Naval, Madrid, MAS. (Middle) Columbus mosaic © Peter Christopher.

Endpapers: Theodor de Bry, 1594. Courtesy of Mansell Collection.

1 *La Caravelle di Colombo*. Nineteenth-century fresco in Villa de Albertis, Genoa, © Frederico Arborio Mella, INDEX, Florence.

2-3 *12.X.1492* by Antonio Brugada. Museo Naval, Madrid, MAS.

5 From Columbus's *First Letter to His Sovereigns*. Basle, 1493. Ancient Art and Architecture Collection.

6 *Columbus* by Sebastiano del Piombo. The Metropolitan Museum of Art, Gift of J. Pierpont Morgan, 1900.

9 The Bettmann Archive.

10 The Bettmann Archive.

CHAPTER ONE

19 The Bettmann Archive.

20 (Top left) Sixteenth-century painting, Scala/Art Resource, (Top right) *La Virgen de Cristóbal Colón*, Anonymous, Museo Lázaro, Madrid, MAS, (Middle, left) *Columbus* by Sir Anthony More, Hulton Picture Library, (Middle, right) 1671 engraving, Mansell Collection, (Bottom left) *Le Llegada de Colón a America*. Archivo Oronoz, Madrid, (Bottom, right) *Cristoforo Colombo*, attributed to Ghirlandaio, Prado Museum, Madrid, INDEX.

20-21 *Columbus* by Emile Lasalle. Bibl. Columbina, Sevilla.

CHAPTER TWO

26-27 *Genoa 1461*. INDEX, Florence.

30-31 Map by Jack McMaster. © Madison Press Books.

32-33 *Triumphal return of Ferdinand of Aragon's Ships*. Pinacoteca de Capodimante, Naples, Archivo AISA, Barcelona.

33 (Inset) *Battle of Lepanto*. National Maritime Museum, Greenwich.

34 Taken from *Voyage d'Outremer*. Bibliotheque Nationale, Paris.

35 (Top) *Mohammed II* by Bellini. National Portrait Gallery, London.

36-37 "Veduto di Chios." from G. Braun's *Civitate Orbum Terrarum*. INDEX, Florence.

37 (Top Right) Mastic print, Korais Library, Chios.

38 From Jean Froissert's *Chroniques* (ca. 1460) Bibliotheque Nationale, Paris.

CHAPTER THREE

40-41 *Departure from Lisbon* by Theodor de Bry. Giraudon/Art Resource.

46 *Prince Henry the Navigator* by Nuno Gonçalves. Giraudon/Art Resource.

48 Map by Jack McMaster. © Madison Press Books.

48-49 *English Ship Running to a Rocky Coast* by Tobias Flessiers. National Maritime Museum, Greenwich.

54 Map by Jack McMaster. © Madison Press Books.

57 Detail from Cantino Planisphere, 1502, Giancarlo Costa, INDEX.

58 Library of Congress.

58-59 *Leif Erickson Discovers America* by Christian Krohg. National Gallery, Oslo.

59 (Top, left) Malak Photographs Ltd., Ottawa.

CHAPTER FOUR

69 G. Vasari. Detail of mural showing Toscanelli in the Palazzo Vecchio. INDEX.

70 *John II*. Kunstarchiv, Vienna.

72-73 *Odyssey* illustration, Archivo Oronoz.

73 Map by Jack McMaster. © Madison Press Books.

CHAPTER FIVE

74 (Inset) *Llegada de Colón a La Rábida*. Archivo Oronoz.

79 Painting from La Rábida © P. Christopher.

80 (Top) *Virgen de los Reyes Católicos* by Francisco Gallego. Museo del Prado, Madrid, MAS, (Bottom) Hernando de Talavera. Patrimonio Nacional, Madrid.

81 (Top) *Virgen de los Reyes Católicos* by Francisco Gallego. Museo del Prado, Madrid, MAS, (Bottom) *Diego de Deza*. Museo del Prado, Madrid, MAS.

82 *Queen Isabella and Columbus* by O'Neill. Bridgeman Art Library.

88 *Batalla de la Higueruela*. Patrimonio Nacional, Madrid, MAS.

90 *Surrender of King Boabdil*. MAS.

95 *Isabel La Católica—Reina de España* by Juan de Flandes. Museo del Prado, Madrid, MAS.

96-97 *Auto de Fé presidido por Santa Domingo de Guzmán* by Pedro Burruguete. Museo de Prado, Madrid, MAS.

97 Taken from *Nuremberg Chronicle*. British Library.

BIBLIOGRAPHY

PRIMARY SOURCES

(Works where several translations and/or editions have been consulted appear without place and year of publication.)

Anglería, Pedro Mártir de. *Décadas.*

Bernáldez, Andrés. *Memoria del reinado de los reyes catolicos.*

Casa, Fray Bartolomé de las. *El libro de la primera navegacíon.* (Extracts from the journal of Christopher Columbus on his discovery voyage).

——. *Historia de las Indias.*

Chaves, Alonso de. *Espejo de navegantes.*

Colón, Hernándo. *The Life of the Admiral Christopher Columbus by His Son.* Translated by Benjamin Keen. New Jersey, 1959.

Gómara, Francisco López de. *Historia general de las Indias.*

Navarrete, Martin Fernández de. *Colección de los viages y descubrimientos que hicieron por mar los Españoles desde fines del siglo XV.*

Oviedo, Gonzalo Fernández de. *Los viajes de Cristóbal Colón.*

SECONDARY SOURCES

Fernandez-Armesto, Felipe. *Before Columbus: Exploration and Colonisation from the Mediterranean to the Atlantic 1229-1492.* London, 1987.

——. *Columbus and the Conquest of the Impossible.* London, 1974.

——. *Ferdinand and Isabella.* London, 1975.

Jane, Cecil (ed.). *The Four Voyages of Columbus.* New York, 1988.

Martinez-Hidalgo, Jose. *Columbus's Ships.* Mass., 1966.

Morison, Samuel Eliot. *Admiral of the Ocean Sea.* Boston, 1942.

——. *The European Discovery of America: The Northern Voyages.* New York, 1971.

——. (trans. and ed.). *Journals and Other Documents on the Life and Voyages of Christopher Columbus.* New York, 1963.

Nunn, G.E. *The Geographical Conceptions of Christopher Columbus.* New York, 1924.

Parry, J.H. *The Discovery of the Sea.*

Taviani, Paolo Emilio. *Christopher Columbus: The Grand Design.* London, 1985.

OTHER USEFUL SOURCES

Argenti, Philip. *The Occupation of Chios by the Genoese.* Cambridge, 1958.

Bathe, Basil W. *Seven Centuries of Sea Travel.* 1972.

Bent, James T. "The Lords of Chios." *English Historical Review,* July 1889.

Bensusan, S.L. *Home Life in Spain.* London, 1910.

Bone, Gertrude. *Days in Old Spain.* London, 1938.

Bradford, Ernle. *Southward the Caravels.* London, 1961.

——. *The Great Siege.* London, 1964.

——. *Mediterranean: Portrait of a Sea.* London, 1971.

——. *Companion Guide to the Greek Islands.* London, 1983.

Boorstin, Daniel J. *The Portuguese Discoverers.* Lisbon, 1987.

Braudel, Fernand. *The Mediterranean.* London, 1972.

Brønsted, Johannes. *The Vikings.* London, 1960.

Calvert, Albert. *The Merchant of Prato.* London, 1957.

Cervantes, Miguel de. *Don Quixote.* Translated by Walter Starkie. New York, 1964.

Conte, Anna del. *Gastronomy of Italy.* London, 1987.

Corry, John. *A History of Bristol.* London, 1816.

Davey, Richard. "The Boyhood and Youth of Columbus." *The National Review,* (1892-93) Vol. XX.

Elbl, Malcolm. *The Portuguese Caravel and European Shipbuilding.* Lisbon, 1985.

Elliott, J.H. *Imperial Spain 1469-1716.* London, 1972.

Elton, Charles I. *The Career of Columbus.* London, 1892.

Fotheringham, J.K. "Genoa and the Fourth Crusade." *English Historical Review,* January 1910.

Garden, Robert W. *The City of Genoa.* London, 1908.

Graham-Campbell, J. & D. Kidd. *The Vikings.* London, 1980.

Gwynne, Paul. *The Guadalquivir.* London, 1912.

Hakluyt Society. *Europeans in West Africa 1450-1560.* London.

Hale, J.R. *Renaissance Europe.* London, 1971.

——. *Renaissance Exploration.* London, 1968.

Hare, Christopher. *A Queen of Queens and the Making of Spain*. London, 1906.

Helps, Arthur. *The Life of Columbus, the Discoverer of America*. London, 1869.

Hewett, Captain J.F. Napier. *Settlements on the West Coast of Africa*. London, 1862.

Highfield, J.R. (ed.). *Spain in the Fifteenth Century*. London, 1972.

Houben, H.H. *Christopher Columbus: The Tragedy of a Discoverer*. London, 1935.

Irving, Washington. *A Chronicle of the Conquest of Granada*. New York, 1894.

Koning, Hans. *Columbus: His Enterprise*. New York, 1965.

Landström, Björn. *Columbus*. Stockholm, 1967.

Lockhart, J.L. & S.B. Schwartz. *Early Latin America*. Cambridge, 1983.

MacNutt, F.A. *Bartholomew de las Casas*. New York, 1909.

Madariaga, Salvador de. *Christopher Columbus*. London, 1979.

Merrien, Jean. *Christopher Columbus: the Mariner and the Man*. Translated by Maurice Michael. London, 1958.

Miller, William. "The Genoese in Chios 1346-1566." *English Historical Review*, July 1915.

Morton, H.V. *A Traveller in Italy*. London, 1964.

Nawrath, Alfred. *Iceland*. Berne, 1959.

Oakeshott, Ewart. *European Arms and Armour*. London, 1980.

Oliveira Marques, A.H. de. *Daily Life in Portugal in the Late Middle Ages*. Wisconsin, 1971.

Parry, J.A. *The Discovery of South America*. London, 1979.

Pike, Ruth. *Aristocrats and Traders*. London, 1972.

———. *Enterprise and Adventure*. New York, 1966.

Pillement, George. *Unknown Spain*. London, 1967.

Polo, Marco. *The Travels*. Translated by Ronald Latham. London, 1958.

Pritchett, V.S. *The Spanish Temper*. London, 1954.

Quinn, D.B. *North American Discovery*. New York, 1971.

———. *England and the Discovery of America, 1481-1620*. London, 1974.

———. "John Day and Columbus." *Geographic Journal*, June 1967.

———. "The Argument for the English Discovery of America between 1480 and 1494." *Geographic Journal*, June 1961.

Ruddock, Alwyn A. *Italian Merchant Shipping in Southampton 1270-1600*. Southampton, 1951.

Runciman, Steven. *The Fall of Constantinople 1453*. Cambridge, 1965.

Sanceau, Elaine. *The Perfect Prince*. Porto, 1959.

Scammell, G.V. *The World Encompassed*. London, 1981.

Shirley, Rodney W. *The Mapping of the World*. London, 1983.

Sismondi, J.C.L. *The History of the Italian Republics in the Middle Ages*. London, ca. 1830.

Skelton, R.A. *Explorers' Maps*. London, 1958.

Stefansson, Vilhjalmur. *Ultima Thule*. London, 1942.

Stephens, H.M. *Portugal*. London, 1908.

Tannahill, Reay. *Food in History*. New York, 1989.

Taylor, E.G.R. "Columbus the Navigator?" *Journal of the Institute of Navigation*, April 1961.

———. "The Navigating Manual of Columbus" *Journal of the Institute of Navigation*, January 1952.

Thomas, Hugh. *Madrid: A Traveller's Companion*. London, 1988.

Vignaud, H. *Toscanelli and Columbus*. London, 1902.

Vaussard, Maurice. *Daily Life in Eighteenth Century Italy*. London, 1964.

Walsh, William Thomas. *Isabella of Spain*. London, 1931.

Waters, David W. *The Art of Navigation in England in Elizabethan and Early Stuart Times*. London, 1958.

Whelpton, Eric. *A Concise History of Italy*. London, 1964.

Wroth, Lawrence C. *The Way of a Ship*. Portland, 1937.

INDEX

Design and Art Direction: Ralph Tibbles Design Inc.

Editorial Director: Hugh M. Brewster

Project Editor: Ian R. Coutts

Editorial Assistance: Rick Archbold

Shelley Tanaka

Production Director: Susan Barrable

Production Assistance: Donna Chong

Maps and Diagrams: Jack McMaster

Typography: On-line Graphics

Color Separation: la cromolito

Printing and Binding: Arnoldo Mondadori Editore

Columbus: For Gold, God and Glory
was produced by Madison Press Books
under the direction of Albert E. Cummings